Alamo Almanac & Book of Lists

William R. Chemerka

EAKIN PRESS ★ Austin, Texas

For my wife, Deborah

FIRST EDITION

Copyright © 1997
By William R. Chemerka

Published in the United States of America
By Eakin Press
A Division of Sunbelt Media, Inc.
P.O. Box 90159 / Austin, Tx 78709

2 3 4 5 6 7 8 9

ISBN 1-57168-150-7

Library of Congress Cataloging-in-Publication Data

Chemerka, William R.
    The Alamo almanac & book of lists / by William R. Chemerka
        p.   cm.
    Includes bibliographical references.
    ISBN 1-57168-150-7
    1. Alamo (San Antonio, Tex.)--Siege, 1836--Miscellanea.   2. Texas--
-History--Revolution, 1835-1836--Miscellanea.   I. Title.
F390.C5   1997
976.4'03--dc21   97-2623
                                                              CIP

Contents

From the Author

The Alamo Almanac & Book of Lists features three main sections: 1) an introduction to the Texas Revolution and the Siege and Battle of the Alamo, 2) an alphabetical section that contains historical and popular culture entries from Juan Abamillo, Alamo defender, to ZZ Top, the Texas-based rock band, and 3) the Lists section.

The primary sources for the alphabetical section came from Alamo book titles; however, when appropriate a periodical or newspaper article was used. General biographies on such individuals as David Crockett and William Barret Travis, for example, were not included.

Many of the entries are followed by a "See" for further reference identification. Most of the book titles identified remain in print. To be sure, the author acknowledges that in a number of instances other titles can easily be substituted for the identified ones.

A complete set of *The Alamo Journal,* the official publication of The Alamo Society, is held at the Daughters of the Republic Library at the Alamo in San Antonio, Texas. Anyone interested in a subscription to *The Alamo Journal* can contact the author in care of the publisher.

The author welcomes comments, corrections, clarifications and, above all, additions to *The Alamo Almanac & Book of Lists.* Please contact the author c/o Eakin Press, P.O. Drawer 90159, Austin, TX 78709-0159.

WILLIAM R. CHEMERKA

The Alamo garrison in 1836 and its three principal heroes
(L–R): Davy Crockett, James Bowie, and William Barrett Travis. Illustration by Joseph Musso

Preface

"Remember the Alamo!"

That passionate phrase, first shouted by avenging soldiers in Sam Houston's army at the Battle of San Jacinto some six weeks after the fall of the Alamo, has resonated ever since in prose, poetry, song, and film. After all, the Siege and Battle of the Alamo is a remarkable episode in the annals of history. But the story of the famous mission-fortress has developed along two interrelated paths: The first one is the historical centerpiece of the Texas Revolution, a scene of defiance, bravery, and sacrifice; the other is a source of artistic creativity, commercialism, and, at times, irreverence.

Frequently over the last one hundred and sixty years the Alamo of history has merged with the Alamo of popular culture. At times, the result of this socio-historical union has been the perpetuation of myth and the distortion of the historical process. A number of authors have attempted to clarify the Alamo story by carefully differentiating between the two aforementioned paths, but the popular perception of what happened during those fateful thirteen days in 1836 is still obscured by larger than life characters, daring deeds, and visual imagery. To be sure, a more complete story of the Siege and Battle of the Alamo has yet to be written. As James W. Davidson and Mark H. Lytle wrote in their essential work, *After the Fact; The Art of Historic Detection,* "the past is not history; only the raw material of it." Fortunately, more "raw material" about the Alamo and its participants is being collected, organized, studied, and evaluated every year by both professional and amateur researchers.

The story of the Alamo is unique, exciting, awesome, stirring, inspirational, tragic, meaningful, significant, and, of course, memorable. Much has been written about the Shrine of Texas Liberty and certainly much more will be written about it. This humble volume helps sort out many of the people, organizations, and creative works that have shaped the story of the Alamo over the centuries. Consider *The Alamo Almanac & Book of Lists* as a guide to what has been produced to date.

"Remember the Alamo!"

WILLIAM R. CHEMERKA
March 1997

Acknowledgments

Any book that calls itself a compilation, an anthology, a collection, or in this case an "almanac and book of lists," certainly must acknowledge all of those titles, whether they are books, films, songs, or other artistic creations. As such, this volume is organized in such a way as to identify those individuals who added to the legendary story of the Alamo. This book identifies many of them; however, the reader should seek out their original works for a more comprehensive appreciation of the Alamo's legacy.

In gathering appropriate information for this book, a number of individuals immediately come to mind. The staff of the Daughters of the Republic of Texas Library at the Alamo were most gracious in providing assistance. Library assistant Linda Edwards must be cited for her courteous professionalism with regards to my research requests. And library assistant Sally Koch deserves special mention for her attentive and responsive research assistance, especially during my 1995 visit to the Alamo. Thanks also to Martha Utterback and her associates who helped secure some of the photo images that grace the following pages. The Daughters of the Republic of Texas, the official custodians of the Alamo, and former Alamo curator Wallace Saage supplied important statistical data for both the "Almanac" and "Lists" section of this book. Former Alamo curator Charles J. Long was decidedly generous with his time and contributions. Thanks also to Dorothy Reed Black for her efforts.

Linda Peterson, Photography Services Coordinator at the University of Texas at Austin's Center for American History, and her associates, were most helpful in allowing the Governor Dolph Brisco Alamo Daguerreotype image to be reprinted in this volume. She was kind enough to point out that a reversed image of the original would "make better visual sense" to the readers. Her suggestion was, of course, followed.

Douglas C. Beach, President of Rivertheatre Associates, and the administrative staff of the IMAX® Theater in San Antonio, Texas were most generous for providing the photo of Gen. Santa Anna and his staff from *Alamo . . . The Price of Freedom.*

Fellow members of the Alamo Society provided a wealth of significant information through their previously published efforts in the *Alamo Journal* and other publications. Bill Groneman, who penned *Alamo Defenders*, buttressed the roster of Alamo couriers and noncombatants. Thomas Ricks Lindley provided information on the roll call of the Alamo garrison and other related topics.

Additional Alamo Society members who made important contributions to the "Lists" section include David Zucker, Dr. Murray Weissmann, "Texas" Bob Reinhardt, and Frank Thompson. Robert Weil provided the cover photograph.

Gary Zaboly provided several excellent illustrations, all of which previously graced the pages of *The Alamo Journal*, including several covers. And Rod Timanus created the two Alamo battle plan diagrams. Other Alamo Society artists who provided original works include Craig Covner, Joseph Musso, Anthony DeSesni, and John Bourdage. Covner also augmented the "Alamo Chronology" with a number of important inclusions.

Other Alamo Society members who provided assistance of one kind or another include Andrew Oren, Edward Dubravsky, Roger Ross, C. Glenn Nolan, John Berky, Bob Carmignani, and Donald Vicaro.

Thanks also to fellow educator William O'Hea, who provided me with the necessary time and assistance to complete my first draft.

Of course, special thanks goes to Fess Parker, star of *Davy Crockett, King of the Wild Frontier*, for his contribution to the "Lists" section. I became interested in the Alamo when I saw Fess Parker in "Davy Crockett at the Alamo," the third part of Walt Disney's Crockett trilogy, on February 23, 1955. His characterization was inspirational! I must thank Fess for his contributions to *The Alamo Journal* and his participation in the 1994 Alamo Society Symposium in San Antonio, Texas.

It would be inappropriate for me not to thank Eakin Press, which initially expressed interest in my idea for this book.

Above all, I must thank my wife, Deborah, who was interested in the Alamo (at least Davy Crockett's participation in it) long before she met me. She has accompanied me to Texas on several occasions over the years, frequently assisting me in my research. We both believe that the Alamo is indeed a shrine.

As a teacher of American History for the past twenty-five years, I have conducted hundreds of classes about the Alamo and its participants. As a matter of fact, I'm reminded of the Alamo every day as I drive to Madison High School in Madison, New Jersey, past Burnet Road (New Jersey-born David G. Burnet was the first president of the Republic of Texas; his wife, Hannah, was born several miles from my home).

On an emotional level, my inspiration for this book comes from the defenders of the Alamo who gave their lives so that others might enjoy liberty and independence. To be sure, the price of freedom is not free.

"Remember the Alamo!"

"Yes, my friends, they preferred to die a thousand times than to live under the yoke of a tyrant."

Juan Seguin
February 25, 1837

INTRODUCTION

The Texas Revolution

"Our manifest destiny [is] to overspread the continent allotted by Providence for the free development of our yearly multiplying millions."

John L. O'Sullivan
1845

Any understanding of Manifest Destiny must include an appreciation of the Texas Revolution (1835–36) and its most epic event: the Siege and Battle of the Alamo. In 1835 the United States looked westward with more than mere fanciful fascination. Indeed, the land west of the Mississippi River represented an opportunity for imperialist-like exploitation. Westward expansionism in the early nineteenth century was closely associated with the aspirations of rugged individuals — pioneers, homesteaders, and ranchers. The abundance of Western land became a beacon to generations of Americans. To be sure, the Andrew Jackson administration was also interested in expansion, but not to the extent that it would reach after 1845, when territorial acquisition "from sea to shining sea" became the most important foreign policy objective of the United States.

Prior to 1836 the flag of Texas was the flag of the Mexican government, which had won its independence from Spain in 1821. At that time, Texas was a land of economic opportunity, but it lacked ample capital, a skilled labor force, and, most importantly, an entrepreneurial class. In order to promote that opportunity and help develop Texas further, Mexico offered liberal land grants to those from the United States

1

who would settle in the lands west of the Sabine River. As early as 1821 American families had settled in Spanish Texas under authority granted to Stephen F. Austin, whose father, Moses, had initially requested a colonial grant from the Spanish authorities a year earlier. These first enterprising Anglo families numbered in the hundreds; Mexico wanted thousands.

As a result, Mexico offered 177 acres of land to farmers and 4,428 acres to ranchers. Furthermore, Mexico stated that no central taxes would be levied for six years. But the government in Mexico City identified several restrictions which accompanied the generous land grants: Anglo immigrants would have to swear allegiance to Mexico, convert to Roman Catholicism, and pledge not to utilize slave labor. The restrictions may have seemed strict to some, but most newcomers did not mind. In fact, for several years Mexico did not vigorously enforce the restrictions. As a result, Americans indeed came by the thousands. To the delight of Mexico, they brought with them their farming, ranching, and entrepreneurial skills. But they also brought with them such American characteristics as representative democracy, private property, the profit motive, freedom of enterprise, and the "peculiar institution," slavery.

By the end of the decade, the few thousand or so Mexicans in Texas were outnumbered nearly seven to one by the growing Anglo population. As a matter of fact, the number of slaves in Texas nearly equaled the native Mexican population. Texas was rapidly developing, but not in the way that the Mexican government had envisioned.

Mexico, however, was quick to act. Legislation passed on April 6, 1830, curbed further colonization from the United States. In addition, the new laws forbade the importation of slaves and levied taxes. Activists among the Anglos, the so-called Texians, initiated a revolt to separate themselves from the neighboring state of Coahuila. Random armed skirmishes between Texian settlers and Mexican soldiers broke out in places like Anahuac and Velasco. Even Stephen F. Austin was imprisoned in Mexico City in 1833 after he pleaded for an independent Texas — at least independent from Coahuila.

Sam Houston, who arrived in Texas at this time to conduct peace talks with the Comanches for President Jackson, placed the local squabbling within a larger framework. Writing to the chief executive, Houston observed: "The people of Texas are determined to form a State Government and separate from Coahuila, and unless Mexico is soon restored to order and the Constitution revived and re-enacted, the Province of Texas will remain separate from the Confederacy of Mexico. If Texas is desirable to the United States, it is now in the most favorable attitude perhaps that it can be to obtain it on fair terms."

The conflicts of the early 1830s gave way to a revolutionary movement fueled, in part, by the dictatorship of Mexican General Antonio Lopez de Santa Anna, who forcefully suppressed a democratic revolt in Zacatecas in 1834.

An emotional American press zealously echoed Houston's earlier sentiments. Noted the Philadelphia *Courier* about a New York City pro-Texas rally: "Texas, Texas. Crowded meetings and gun-powder speeches, calling down vengeance upon the oppressors of the Texonians, is the order of the day." Funds were privately raised for the liberty-threatened Texians, and volunteers headed west.

Although sympathetic to Texian concerns, President Jackson remained diplomatically neutral. He ordered Secretary of State John Forsyth in November 1835 to alert his district attorneys to curb intervention by individual Americans in Mexico's domestic problems. But Texian aspirations were not as uniform as readers of the Eastern press may have believed. The Texian revolutionaries, like their American counterparts in 1775, were divided. One faction of rebels wanted a guarantee that its rights as Mexican citizens under the liberal Mexican Constitution of 1824 would be restored. Others, however, wanted a complete break from Santa Anna's dictatorship.

From October 15 until November 1, 1835, the rebel government was the San Felipe-based General Council, headed by president R. R. Royal. Among their bold efforts, the ad hoc Council formed volunteer ranging companies, sought financial aid from U.S. citizens, and encouraged privateers to attack Mexican ships. The General Council then yielded to the more formal Consultation, whose delegates elected Dr. Branch T. Archer of Brazoria as president. The delegates, who hailed from a dozen Texian districts, opted at the time for a restoration of rights, not independence.

Nevertheless, they prepared to fight Santa Anna, whom Mina delegate D. C. Barrett called the "Usurper." Noted Barrett: "We declare and resolve that we are . . . at war with Santa Anna and his supporters . . . ." By mid-November the delegates selected Stephen F. Austin as a commissioner to the United States. Henry Smith was elected governor, and Sam Houston was appointed commander of the embryonic regular army.

Although the revolutionary government was finally organized, the first shots of this war had actually been fired a month earlier at Gonzales when a mounted Mexican unit commanded by Lt. Francisco Castañeda was thwarted in its attempt to retrieve an artillery piece from an armed group of Texians who defiantly challenged the attackers to "Come and Take It."

At the time, Castañeda and all other Mexican units in Texas were under the command of Gen. Martin Perfecto de Cos, Santa Anna's brother-in-law, who had been based in San Antonio since September with over one thousand men and twenty-one artillery pieces. Cos was entrusted by Santa Anna to curb the growing rebellion by capturing the rebel leaders and disarming the others. However, the armed Texians had plans of their own.

In the early morning hours of October 10, a Texian company under the command of Capt. George M. Collinsworth skirmished with a small Mexican detachment at Goliad and captured the fortress.

Several weeks later on October 28, a force of nearly one hundred Texians under the command of James Bowie defeated a larger Mexican unit at Mission Concepcion outside of San Antonio. On November 6, less than four dozen Texians curbed an attack by a Mexican force nearly twice their size at Fort Lipantitlan on the Nueces River. A momentum of martial achievement seemed to pervade the Texian camps.

However, not all Texian military operations were successful during the autumn of 1835. An attempt to capture the Mexican port of Tampico in November was a complete failure. The small attacking force was captured and sentenced to death. One of President Andrew Jackson's diplomats in Mexico City, George R. Robertson, attempted to purchase the freedom of the twenty-seven condemned men but was rebuked by the authorities. On December 14 all of the captured men, some of whom hailed from European nations, were shot to death.

Only five days before the executions, the Texians scored their most important military success of the young rebellion. A force under Gen. Edward Burleson stationed near San Antonio decided to attack the Mexican settlement on December 5, 1835. The assault was initiated as a two-prong movement led by Colonels Francis W. "Frank" Johnson and Ben Milam. The fighting took place over several days as Mexican and Texians battled from street to street and house to house before Cos capitulated on December 9. The Texians won control of the town and its nearby mission-fortress, the Alamo. But the victory was not without its costs. Some three dozen Texians were wounded in the Battle of Béxar; six were killed. Among the dead was the 43-year-old Milam.

Burleson's terms to Cos were generous. He requested that the Mexican soldiers respect the Constitution of 1824, abandon Texas, and pledge not to return. By December 25, Cos' army, *sans* artillery, and a portion of its supplies, crossed the Rio Grande on its return to Mexico City. But the Texian victory was marred by departing volunteers who longed for home. Others joined an ill-fated military scheme to capture Matamoros. By January of 1836 the size of Texian forces in Béxar numbered just over one hundred men.

Cos' defeat was the catalyst which prompted Santa Anna, the self-proclaimed "Napoleon of the West," to invade Texas, reclaim San Antonio, and suppress the revolution. Santa Anna planned to personally lead the army. By late December, the Army of Operations, over four thousand men strong, headed north. On January 20, 1836, Santa Anna ordered his second-in-command, Gen. Vicente Filisola and Gen. Ramirez y Sesma, to "stop all communications with Bejar, without permitting

General Santa Anna. Illustration by John Bourdage.

the passage of food supplies, only allowing trustworthy and discerning spies to pass, who may be able to tell with certainty the conditions found in that city. . . ."

The Alamo garrison was weakened following the Battle of Béxar when an awkwardly conceived expedition against the Mexican town of Matamoros was authorized by the Texian representative body in San Felipe. The expeditionary force was to be led by James Grant and Frank Johnson, with a sizable number of men under Col. James Neill's command in the Alamo. Although the plan was criticized by Gov. Henry Smith, it went into effect anyway. As a result, men, supplies, and money dwindled to such an extent that the Alamo seemed particularly vulnerable. "The clothing sent here . . . was taken from us by the arbitrary measures of Johnson and Grant, taken from men who endured all the hardships of winter . . . ," wrote Neill to Governor Smith and the Council on January 6, 1836. "I want here, for this garrison, at all times two hundred men, and I think three hundred men, until the repairs and improvement of fortifications are completed. . . ."

Despite the unforgiving winter of 1835-1836, Santa Anna's *soldados* marched onward, reaching the Rio Grande on February 17. There to greet the army was another Mexican brigade, a force of some fifteeen hundred men under command of General Ramirez y Sesma. Within a week, advance units of Sesma reached San Antonio. On February 23, 1836, the Siege of the Alamo had begun. Sesma's soldiers raised a red flag atop the San Fernando church in the town, which signaled that the Alamo's defenders were to receive no quarter — if the Mexicans could breech the mission's walls. Shortly thereafter, Mexican artillery began a relentless pounding of the Alamo.

The Alamo had undergone leadership changes since Cos' surrender in December. Col. James C. Neill, who commanded the beleaguered garrison, left for home for a short leave on February 14 to attend to pressing family health problems. The command of the old Spanish mission was entrusted to Lt. Col. William B. Travis, a 26-year-old South Carolinian, although sentiment among some of the volunteers sided with James Bowie, the 40-year-old Kentuckian who arrived at the Alamo

"North Wall Diggers Under Fire." Illustration by Gary Zaboly.

with discretionary instructions from Gen. Sam Houston to destroy and abandon the Alamo. Some in the 150-man garrison, perhaps, preferred David Crockett, the 49-year-old former congressman, to be commander. However, the famous frontiersman opted for the rank of "high private."

The Alamo defenders were a diverse group. Several were Tejanos, like Juan Abamillo and Toribio Losoya, who were Mexican-born. Others hailed from such countries as Great Britain, Germany, and Denmark. The majority, however, came from the United States. They made their way to Texas from Alabama, Pennsylvania, Massachusetts, Tennessee, Maine, New Jersey, Virginia, and over a dozen other states. Some had lived in Texas for several years, like George Washington Cottle of Missouri. Others, like William H. Fontleroy of Kentucky, had arrived only months earlier. In early 1836, however, they all considered themselves Texians.

Although the Alamo had physically deteriorated since its secularization in 1793, Colonel Neill and engineer Green Jameson fortified the old mission and strengthened some of its more glaring weak spots, namely the lengthy opening between the church and the South Wall. And the old adobe and stone walls were augmented with twenty-one artillery pieces, making the Alamo one of the largest artillery parks in North America at the time. Guns ranging in size from two small brass pieces and several workhorse three-and four-pounders to an impressive eighteen-pounder punctuated the walls and main courtyard. At least one artillery piece supported the palisade area. The roofless Alamo church's interior was transformed into an elongated dirt and stone gun ramp featuring a platform mounted at the building's elevated eastern side. Three guns protected the back of the old church.

Travis did not wait for the Mexicans to attack. He sent out numerous messengers with pleas for help. Travis' letter of February 24 is memorable for its determination, spirit, and singularity of purpose. "I shall never surrender or retreat," wrote Travis. "Victory or Death." Santa Anna would have it no other way.

Commandancy of the Alamo
Bexar, Feby 24th, 1836

To the People of Texas and All
Americans in the World—

Fellow Citizens and Compatriots:

I am besieged by a thousand or
more of the Mexicans under Santa
Anna. I have sustained a continu-
al Bombardment and cannonade for
24 hours and have not lost a
man. The enemy has demanded surrender at discretion, otherwise the
garrison is to be put to the sword,
if the fort is taken. I have an-
swered the demand with a cannon
shot, & our flag still waves proudly from the wall. I shall never
surrender or retreat. Then, I call on
you in the name of Liberty, of pa-
triotism, and everything dear to the
American character, to come to our
aid with all dispatch. The enemy is
receiving reinforcements daily and
will no doubt increase to three or
four thousand in four or five days.
If this call is neglected I am determined to sustain myself as long
as possible and die like a soldier

who never forgets what is due his honor and that of his country.

Victory or Death

William Barrett Travis
Lt. Col. Commanding

P.S. The Lord is on our side. When the enemy appeared in sight we had not three bushels of corn. We have since found in deserted houses 80 to 90 bushels & got into the walls 20 or 30 head of Beeves.

During the thirteen-day siege, a small relief force from Gonzales arrived, increasing the size of the garrison to over two hundred defenders. However, the number of active combatants was reduced due to illness and disease. James Bowie was probably one of the more seriously ill men. Still, they held out. Perhaps Fannin would arrive with his force from Goliad, they thought. Perhaps Houston's army was not far off. What of other volunteer units? A letter dated March 1 from Maj. R. M. Williamson pledged more than six hundred reinforcements. "For God's sake, hold out until we can assist you," wrote Williamson.

Unknown to the Alamo defenders, on March 2, 1836, Texas formally declared itself an independent republic at a meeting of delegates to a General Convention at Washington-on-the-Brazos.

"View of the Alamo's southern defenses." Illustration by Gary Zaboly.

Santa Anna decided the Siege of the Alamo had gone on long enough. On the afternoon of March 5 the general created his plan of attack for the next morning. His army would assault the Alamo in four columns, led by General Cos, Col. Francisco Duque, Col. Jose Maria Romero and Col. Juan Morales, respectively. In order to scale some of the Alamo's massive walls, several *soldados* were issued scaling ladders and tools.

Santa Anna's orders read: "The first column will be commanded by Gen. Don Martin Perfecto Cos, and in his absence, by myself.

"The Permanent Battalion of Aldama (except the company of grenadiers) and the three right centre companies of the Active Battalion of San Luis, will compose the first column.

"The second column will be commanded by Colonel Don Francisco Duque, and in his absence, by General Don Manuel Fernandez Castrillon: it will be composed of the Active Battalion of Toluca (except the company of Grenadiers) and the three remaining centre companies of the active Battalion of San Luis.

"The third column will be commanded by Colonel Jose Maria Romero, and in his absence, by Colonel Mariano Salas; it will be composed of the Permanent Battalions of Matamoros and Jimenes.

"The fourth column will be commanded by Colonel Juan Morales, and in his absence, by Colonel Jose Minon; it will be composed of the light companies of the Battalions of Matamoros and Jimenes, and of the Active Battalion of San Luis."

Among other details in Santa Anna's secret orders was the instruction: "The arms, principally the bayonets, should be in perfect order."

Before dawn on March 6, 1836, some thousand or more Mexican infantrymen, some shouting *"Viva Santa Anna"* as the buglers played the blood-curdling "Deguello," attacked the Alamo's walls.

Despite the darkness, Alamo artillery and shoulder arms fire generated enough firepower to alter the assault routes of all four attacks. Without hesitation, the Mexican columns re-

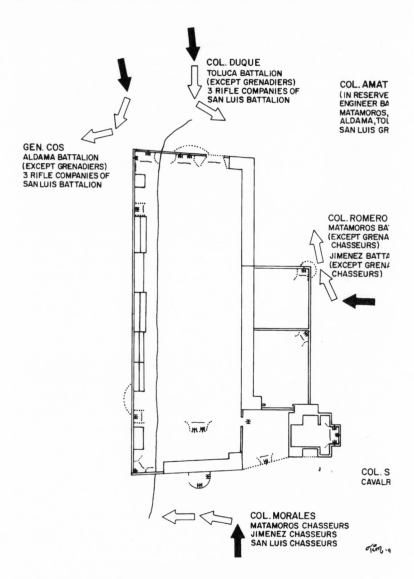

Santa Anna's initial assault was thwarted by the Alamo defenders.
Diagram by Rod Timanus.

formed and pressed the assault. Texian muzzleloaders had forced an unplanned concentration of the Cos, Duque (Castrillon commanding following Duque's death), and Romero columns at the North Wall. The Texians were also effective in shifting Morales' column away from the wooden palisade. Morales' men regrouped near the southwest corner of the compound at the base of the Alamo's eighteen-pound gun and charged again.

The battle raged on as musket and rifle fire filled the air with smoke. Unable to scale the Alamo walls with the inital four-column assault, Santa Anna ordered in the reserve troops under Col. Augustin Amat. The respected Zapadores Battalion and five grenadier companies under Amat helped the struggling infantry to breach the North Wall. Simultaneously, many of Cos' men broke through an opening along the northern portion of the West Wall. As a result of Mexican penetration, the Texians immediately abandoned the walls. In less than an hour, the Mexican infantry had command of the Alamo's main courtyard.

By approximately six o'clock in the morning, the remains of the Texian defense were concentrated in the fortified rooms of the Long Barracks and the church. Perhaps a few isolated rooms along the South and West walls also held handfuls of determined defenders, but their fate was sealed. A small number of Texians, including some members of the Tennessee Mounted Volunteers, were isolated in the area immediately in front of the church.

Mexican infantrymen turned Texian artillery around and fired into the wooden doors of the rooms. Each broken door was followed by an assault of *soldados.* Some of the bloodiest fighting of the battle took place in these darkened, smoke-filled rooms.

The final minutes of battle claimed the lives of the last Texian effectives, possibly Crockett and several others, in the courtyard of the church. A few last stands took place in random, isolated rooms in the Long Barracks and inside the church. A number of defenders may have attempted to escape from the defenses; however, they met their fate at the hands

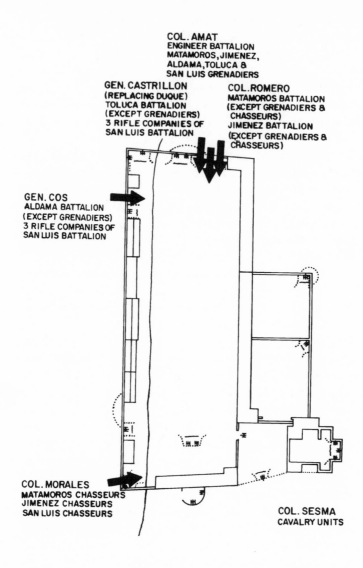

COL. AMAT
ENGINEER BATTALION
MATAMOROS, JIMENEZ,
ALDAMA, TOLUCA &
SAN LUIS GRENADIERS

GEN. CASTRILLON
(REPLACING DUQUE)
TOLUCA BATTALION
(EXCEPT GRENADIERS)
3 RIFLE COMPANIES OF
SAN LUIS BATTALION

COL. ROMERO
MATAMOROS BATTALION
(EXCEPT GRENADIERS &
CHASSEURS)
JIMENEZ BATTALION
(EXCEPT GRENADIERS &
CHASSEURS)

GEN. COS
ALDAMA BATTALION
(EXCEPT GRENADIERS)
3 RIFLE COMPANIES OF
SAN LUIS BATTALION

COL. MORALES
MATAMOROS CHASSEURS
JIMENEZ CHASSEURS
SAN LUIS CHASSEURS

COL. SESMA
CAVALRY UNITS

Mexican soldiers re-fromed and breached the Alamo's outer walls.
Diagram by Rod Timanus.

of Mexican cavalry stationed outside of the Alamo's walls. When it was over, probably two hundred or more Texians lay dead. Several hundred Mexican soldiers were either killed or wounded.

Santa Anna ordered the bodies of the Texian dead to be burned. The remaining women and children non-combatants, including the only Anglo woman, Susannah Dickinson, were allowed to leave unmolested.

The Battle of the Alamo was over. For Santa Anna, the events of March 6, 1836, were "but a small affair," because there were still other military objectives to achieve. A larger Texian force at Goliad, a more formidable fortress, had to be taken. In addition, Juan Seguin's mounted unit had to be captured and other relief columns had to be countered. And Houston's army was still somewhere in the field.

However, on March 20 Fannin surrendered near Coleto Creek to Gen. Jose Urrea, who had previously defeated Texian forces at Agua Dulce, San Patricio, and Refugio. The Texians believed they would be treated as prisoners of war who would eventually be sent to New Orleans. However, on March 27 Santa Anna ordered the execution of Fannin's command, save a handful of doctors, engineers, and mechanics. Nearly four hundred men were executed, although several dozen managed to escape by crossing the San Antonio River.

Santa Anna was finally defeated at San Jacinto on April 21, 1836, as the cries "Remember the Alamo" and "Remember Goliad" were shouted by attacking Texian troops under Houston. Santa Anna and over four thousand of his soldiers were instructed to leave the Republic of Texas and return to Mexico. The Texas Revolution was over. Texas had won its independence.

From 1836 until 1845, Texas remained an independent, sovereign nation. On December 29, 1845, Texas joined the United States of America as the twenty-eighth state.

In the second half of the nineteenth century, the Alamo went through a number of architectural incarnations. The

United States Army built a roof on the church and constructed its unique, hump-like facade. The Confederacy occupied it
during the Civil War, and commercial interests purchased it
later in the century. In the early twentieth century, the Daughters of the Republic of Texas (DRT), primarily through the efforts of two of its members, Adina de Zavala and Clara
Driscoll, rescued the Alamo from commercial oblivion. The
DRT continues to serve as the official custodian of the Alamo
and its 4.2 acres of grounds, which includes a research library
and a gift shop/museum.

During the one hundred-fifty-plus years of Texas statehood, the line between the Alamo of history and the Alamo of
popular culture has been frequently blurred by artists, writers,
poets, tune smiths, filmmakers, political activists, historians,
and cartoonists. Furthermore, the image of the Alamo church
has been exploited by hundreds of commercial enterprises,
each attempting to gain consumer recognition from the most
identifiable historical silhouette, save the Statue of Liberty, in
the United States.

Like all symbols, the Shrine of Texas Liberty has been em-
braced by many and scorned by some. Still, the Alamo remains.
And so do the memories of all who fought there during those
thirteen days of glory in 1836.

Alamo

Chronology

ALAMO CHRONOLOGY

1519 Spain claims section of North America which includes present day Texas.

1716 The Duke of Valero, Spanish viceroy in Mexico City, is asked by Fray Antonio de San Buenaventura y Olivares that the San Francisco Solano mission be moved to the San Antonio area.

1718 Fray Antonio de San Buenaventura y Olivares, who received permission to assume control of an Indian settlement adjacent to San Antonio River, names the new mission San Antonio de Valero, after Saint Anthony of Padua and the Marquis of Valero.

1724 A furious storm destroys the nascent mission's huts. Mission is moved to its present location. Construction begins on the *convento* (friary or "priest's quarters").

1727 Materials are gathered to build church.

1739 Epidemic greatly reduces mission population. Master mason Antonio Tello arrives to design and build "permanent" church.

1744 Foundation work completed, the cornerstone is laid on May 8. In August, master mason Tello flees town after being accused of murder. Construction halts, then continues without a master's guidance.

ca. 1750 Nearing completion, the church collapses totally.

1751 Master mason Hieronymo Ybarra arrives in San

Antonio to finish mission Concepcion and re-build Valero church (the present day Alamo).

1758   Date inscribed on keystone above church door.

ca. 1760   Prompted by the rising militancy of the Apaches and massacre of missionaries by Comanches and Wichitas at San Saba, mission Valero is enclosed in a protective wall of "stone, adobe, and mud."

1762   Indian population at mission recorded as two hundred and seventy-five individuals or seventy-six families.

1763   Spain receives former French territory in America west of the Mississippi River as a result of the Treaty of Paris, which officially ends the Seven Years' War.

1773   Queretarian friars turn over care of Texas missions to those of the college of Zacatecas.

1777   Census indicates only forty-four Indians remaining at San Antonio de Valero.

1785   Last marriage ceremony is performed at mission San Antonio de Valero. Earliest known granting of Valero mission property to an individual: the southwest corner room of the compound to Pedro Charli.

1789   Report states that services have to be held in the sacristy adjoining the still unfinished church, which, due to lack of population and skilled crafts men, cannot be completed.

1793   Mission San Antonio de Valero is secularized, and its land and assets are distributed or transferred.

1800   By secret treaty, Spain cedes Louisiana back to France, with the provison that no English-speaking country should ever gain control of it.

1801   Spanish soldiers, the Segunda Compania Volante

(Second Flying Company) of San Carlos de Parras, garrison the former mission and establish the parish and Pueblo de San Jose y Santiago del *Alamo*. El Alamo was a town near Parras in Mexico where soldiers had been recruited in 1788. The name of the pueblo gradually supplants the original mission name.

1803   Money-hungry Napoleon breaks France's word and sells Louisiana to the United States during Thomas Jefferson's presidency for $15 million.

1805   Former mission friary, or *convento*, is converted to San Antonio's first hospital.

1809   Reports of U. S. troops massing on the Texas-Louisiana border spurs Governor Manuel Salcedo to strengthen fortifications at Béxar, including those of the Alamo. Barracks and guardhouse/jail flanking the South gate are built around this time.

1810   Father Hidalgo foments Mexican independence movement. Extensive repairs to the hospital in the Alamo are completed.

1811   Texas governor Salcedo, a staunch Royalist, announces that government troops, including the Alamo garrison, would be sent to the Rio Grande to meet the rebel threat. Insurrectionists in Béxar cause panic by spreading rumors that Texas is to be abandoned and the Alamo barracks burned. Rebel leader Juan Bautista Casa makes the Alamo his headquarters.

1812   Gutierrez–Magee expedition enters Texas from Louisiana.

1813   The invaders, following several victories against the Spanish, arrive in San Antonio and occupy the Alamo; later they are decimated by Spanish General Arredondo at the Battle of Medina.

1814   Crumbling Indian quarters at Alamo ordered thatched to accommodate troops there.

1816   San Antonio de Béxar is virtually deserted.

1821   Mexico achieves independence from Spain. Conditions improve at Béxar with large number of troops assigned there. Civilian population swells.

1823   Local government petitioned to sell small houses lining Alamo walls as soon as barracks for increased garrison can be constructed.

1824   Mexican constitution provides statehood for Texas.

1825   Alamo garrison commander requests former *convento*-hospital be assigned as permanent quarters, as no new barracks had been built.

1829   Lot and ruined building along the Alamo's west wall deeded to Alexandro Trevino, captain of the Presidial Company of Béxar. Previously, properties along the same wall and north wall were deeded to soldiers of the Company Volante.

1830   Law of 1830 prohibits further legal emigration from the United States.

1834   Santa Anna is elected president of Mexico.

1835   First shots of the Texas Revolution are fired at Gonzales. Gen. Martin Perfecto de Cos occupies, fortifies, then surrenders the Alamo to Texian forces following Battle of Béxar.

1836   Siege and Battle of the Alamo. Texas declares itself independent from Mexico. Following Santa Anna's defeat at San Jacinto, retreating Mexican forces dismantle fortifications at the Alamo and level all single walls.

1837   Ceremonies held for Alamo defenders; some remains are interred.

1840	The city council agrees to sell a Reverend Valdez stone "which is in the wall of the Alamo" at four *reales* per cart load.
1841	Congress of the Republic of Texas declares the Alamo property to be that of the Roman Catholic Church.
1842	Mexican Generals Rafael Vasquez and Adrian Woll invade Texas and occupy San Antonio briefly in March and September.
1845	Company "G," 2nd U. S. Cavalry, is the first United States unit to ocupy the Alamo on October 28, 1845. Texas becomes the twenty-eighth state on December 29, 1845.
1846	Lone Star Republic flag flies for the last time as Texas is officially annexed by the United States on February 16.
1847	U. S. Army assumes control of the Alamo for use as a quartermaster site, but recognizes Catholic church's ownership. Former *convento*-hospital-Long Barracks rebuilt and repurposed by U. S. Army.
1849	Daguerreotype image of ruined church is taken, the earliest known "photo" of the Alamo.
1850	The Alamo's "trademark" parapet design, or famous "hump," is erected during roofing of the reconditioned church by the U. S. Army.
1861	Confederate forces take control of the Alamo after Texas secedes from the United States on February 1.
1865	United States assumes control of the Alamo following end of the Civil War, but Catholic church demands mission be used for German immigrants.
1866	Storm damages former south barrack building.

1871   Remains of south barrack cleared from plaza.

1877   Honore Grenet purchases former Long Barrack building from Catholic church.

1878   Grenet erects "atrocious" lumber "castle" over the Long Barrack, further obliterating what little original construction remained. New quartermaster depot at Fort Sam Houston ready for occupation. When the quartermaster vacates the church building, Grenet obtains a 99-year lease to use it as a warehouse.

1883   State of Texas purchases Alamo church for $20,000 from Catholic church.

1886   Following death of Honore Grenet, entrepreneurs Hugo & Schmeltzer purchase his property at an estate auction for $28,000.

1892   Adina de Zavala, of the De Zavala chapter of the Daughters of the Republic of Texas (DRT), offers to buy Alamo properties from Hugo & Schmeltzer.

1905   Agreement between DRT and Hugo & Schmeltzer to shift ownership of the Alamo is completed. However, lack of fund-raising dollars places sale in jeopardy until the DRT's Clara Driscoll financially intervenes. State legislature authorizes Driscoll's $65,000 purchase (along with other previously raised funds) of the Alamo with the condition that the DRT be designated as the official custodian of the Alamo. Legislature also states that future Alamo improvements must be approved by both DRT and the governor of Texas.

1907   Legal battle between the DRT and the De Zavala chapter over custodianship of the Alamo reaches Harris County court. DRT wins temporary injunction against De Zavala chapter.

1908	Following Adina de Zavala's protest inside Long Barracks, DRT loses injunction.
1909	Texas governor T. M. Campbell assumes control of Alamo during court struggle between DRT and De Zavala chapter.
1910	First Court of Civil Appeals in Galveston sides with DRT's appeal for custodianship. Texas assumes ownership of Alamo with DRT as custodians. DRT begins plans to remove all modern embellishments on Alamo grounds, including the second story of the Long Barracks. De Zavala chapter protests Long Barracks demolition.
1911	Texas governor Oscar J. Colquitt suggests a complete 1836-like restoration of the Alamo contrary to the DRT plan.
1912	Gov. Oscar J. Colquitt removes DRT as custodians of the Alamo. However, DRT wins Fourth Court of Civil Appeals decision, which restores custodianship of the Alamo to the DRT. Architect Alfred Giles proposes 802-foot high Alamo monument.
1913	DRT completes removal of second story of Long Barracks. DRT's proposal to build a Spanish-like architectural wall around the Alamo is criticized by Texas governor Colquitt. After legislature authorizes $5,000 for Alamo improvements, DRT submits unsuccessful legislative draft to eliminate governor from Alamo jurisdiction.
1914	Japan's Shigetka Shiga presents monument honoring Alamo defenders. Shiga saw 1836 struggle as a parallel to 1575 Japanese battle for Nagashino Castle.
1915	DRT establishes maintenance fund which generates approximately $100 a month.

1918   Alamo Mission chapter of DRT plans to raise $2,000 to reroof the Alamo.

1921   New roof completed along with permament electric lighting.

1924   New front door header placed in position.

1925   Replastering effort initiated to prevent sections of Alamo from falling.

1928   San Antonio Public Service Company hooks up gas line to provide the Alamo church with heat.

1931   Texas legislature allocates $150,000 for DRT to purchase land adjacent to the Alamo. Clara Driscoll adds $65,000 to the land-purchasing fund.

1933   Two-year restoration work program commences.

1936   Republic of Texas Centennial Commission authorizes construction of Alamo Cenotaph during Texas Centennial. New Alamo roof completed along with construction of the Alamo Museum and Gift Shop building, acequia, and courtyard well. Flagstone floor inside Alamo church completed.

1938   San Antonio gives Crockett Street firehouse to DRT, which remodels it as Alamo Hall. New Deal's Works Progress Administration conducts restoration work.

1940   Alamo Cenotaph, designed by Pompeo Coppini, is dedicated on November 11, the twenty-second anniversary of the World War I armistice.

1950   Completion of Alamo Library.

1961   Alamo church is hooked up for air conditioning in May, courtesy of General Electric.

1965   General Electric and San Antonio's Public Service

provide exterior lighting to the Alamo and Cenotaph.

1969   Scenes from the comedy *Viva Max* are filmed at the Alamo.

1982   Restoration work begins on Alamo's limestone walls.

1984   An exterior Alamo church scene is filmed for *Pee Wee's Big Adventure.*

1985   January snow storm drops record 13 inches on the Alamo, nearly double the previous all-time record snow fall of 1926. Archaeological dig uncovers bayonet, musket balls and parts, and an eight-inch howitzer shell, among other items.

1986   Alamo Sesquicentennial is commemorated.

1988   Restoration work includes new cedar entry doors and treatment of Alamo's limestone walls. South side door on Alamo church and South Wall guardhouse foundation are uncovered.

1987   Alamo curator Steve Beck says that bus exhaust fumes are damaging the Long Barracks.

1988   Archaeological dig uncovers military hardware, musket balls, and pottery, among other items. Modern Alamo church appears on screen at conclusion of *Alamo . . . The Price of Freedom.*

1989   Extensive restoration work continues on Alamo church, primarily to promote water runoff from the walls. Austin-based National Underwater and Marine Agency (NUMA) conducts first annual Alamo Plaza dig.

1990   Eleven-point Alamo restoration project completed on January 12.

1993   Public discussion proposes restoring Alamo to its 1836 appearance.

1994   Sixth annual Alamo Plaza dig conducted by
            NUMA. *San Antonio Express-News* illustrator Fe-
            lipe Soto creates an extensive drawing of a recre-
            ated 1836-like Alamo Plaza. In October Alamo
            Plaza Study Committee recommends closing
            Alamo Plaza to traffic, protecting all extant struc-
            tures and constructing educational markers.

1995   Extensive cleaning of Alamo church exterior is
            completed. Controversial archaeological dig
            searches for a non-existent Alamo well that sup-
            posedly contained Jim Bowie's hidden treasure.

1997   Alamo continues its post-sesquicentennial atten-
            dance figure of approximately three million visi-
            tors a year. Wall of History erected.

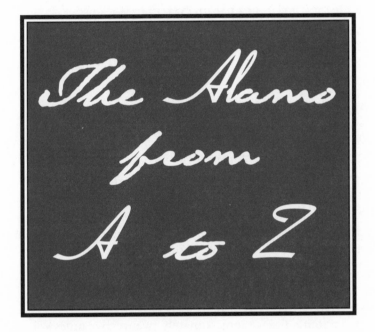

ABAMILLO, JUAN
Tejano sergeant in Capt. Juan Seguin's cavalry company who was killed at the Alamo on March 6, 1836 (see Bill Groneman: *Alamo Defenders*).

"ACROSS THE ALLEY FROM THE ALAMO"
Joe Greene-penned 1947 song which was recorded by Woody Herman (Columbia Records), Stan Kenton (Capital), the Mills Brothers (Decca), the Starlighters (Mercury), and the 3 Suns (Victor).

ADAIR, A. GARLAND
Co-editor (with M. H. Crockett) of the 1956 book *Heroes of the Alamo*, a collection of articles, poems, songs, and photographs about the famous mission-fortress.

AFTER THE ALAMO: THE STORY OF THE MEXICAN WAR
Burt Hirschfeld's 1960 book about the war between the United States and Mexico. In an early section on the War for Texas Independence, the author describes Crockett's death: "A Mexican lieutenant finally dealt him a crashing sword-blow above the right eye, and David Crockett went down."

AGUA DULCE CREEK
Site in South Texas (approximately twenty-five miles south of San Patricio) of military engagement on March 2, 1836, between Mexican cavalry under Brig. Gen. Juan Jose Urrea and some two dozen Texians under James Grant. Grant was killed, along with most of his men, in this skirmish which, coincidentally, took place on the day Texas declared itself independent from Mexico (see Stephen L. Hardin: *Texian Iliad*).

AGUA VERDE
Town in Mexico which supplied cavalrymen for one of seven mounted units stationed at the Alamo in 1835 (see Alwyn Barr: *Texans in Revolt: The Battle for San Antonio, 1835*).

ALAMO
Mission San Antonio de Valero (later known as the Alamo) was founded by the Spanish on May 1, 1718. Construction on the Alamo church that stands today was begun in 1758 fol-

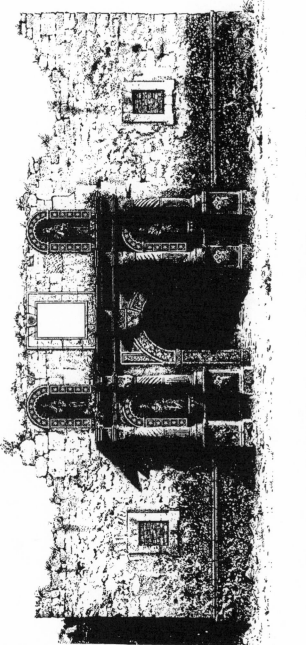

The Alamo church during the thirteen-day 1836 siege. Illustration by Craig Covner.

lowing the laying of the cornerstone on May 8, 1744. However, the structure was never completed, and in 1793 the Catholic church terminated its mission function. The Alamo's name originates either with a Spanish military unit that was stationed there in the early nineteenth century (The Second Flying Company of San Carlos de Parras, which was situated near El Alamo in Coahuila), or the cottonwood trees (*alamo* means cottonwood) that grew near it. An 1803 baptismal entry at the mission recorded the location as *el Alamo*. Following the Battle of Béxar in December 1835, Mexican forces under Gen. Martin Perfecto de Cos surrendered the Alamo to Gen. Edward Burleson. Mexican forces under Gen. Antono Lopez de Santa Anna returned on February 23, 1836, and initiated the thirteen-day siege which culminated in the famous pre-dawn battle on March 6, 1836, in which all the defenders were killed. In the nineteenth century, the Alamo was used by the United States Army as a quartermaster's depot, a Confederate armory, and a commercial warehouse. The property was later acquired by the Daughters of the Republic of Texas, an organization which has served as the official custodian of the Alamo since 1905. It was not until 1960 that the Alamo was designated a national landmark by the federal government (see Daughters of the Republic of Texas: *The Alamo Long Barrack Museum*).

ALAMO
Rock quartet (Ken Woodley, organ and vocals; Larry Rasperry, guitar; Richard Roseborough, drums; and Larry Davis, bass) which released self-titled debut LP in 1971 on Atlantic Records. Barbara Sutherland Lewis created the color art of the modern Alamo church for the band's LP cover.

ALAMO ASSOCIATION
Turn of the century organization. One of the group's committe members, John S. Ford, wrote *Origin and Fall of the Alamo, March 6, 1836* in 1896.

ALAMO CHAIR
Houston-based abstract wood sculptor Adam St. John's 1987 creation which featured an Alamo-shaped back rest. St. John placed a $3,000 price tag on each of the special edition chairs

he created (see "Chairing the Alamo" in *Texas Highways*, January 1988).

ALAMO CITY GUARDS

A local Confederate militia unit commanded by Capt. William M. Edgar which controlled the Alamo during the Civil War (see Daughters of the Republic of Texas: *The Alamo Long Barrack Museum*).

ALAMO DE PARRAS

Town in Mexico which supplied cavalrymen for one of seven mounted units stationed at the Alamo in 1835 (see Alwyn Barr: *Texans in Revolt: The Battle for San Antonio, 1835*).

ALAMO DEFENDERS

Bill Groneman's 1990 volume which features alphabetical biographical sketches of the Alamo's defenders. The volume also includes a section of select letters written by several of the defenders. Of Crockett's death: "David Crockett died fighting during the Battle of the Alamo while defending his assigned area in front of the chapel."

"ALAMO, THE"

Mrs. Stephen F. Austin's undated pamphlet which traces the Siege and Battle of the Alamo. Of Crockett's death: "As the remainder of the garrison stood back of him, reloading and handing him their weapons, Crockett guarded the main door to the chapel until he fell."

ALAMO, THE

Reynold Brown's 1960 painting used for promotional art in conjunction with the release of John Wayne's *The Alamo*. For years this work hung in the Alamo Museum and Gift Shop at the Alamo (see Rod Timanus: "The Battle of the Alamo in Art" in *The Alamo Journal*, #90, February 1994).

ALAMO, THE

Clearvueav's 1993 educational filmstrip about the Siege and Battle of the Alamo. "The Alamo" is one of four audiocassette titles in the Chicago, Illinois-based company's "Protecting Our Liberty" set (part of the five-set *Cornerstones of Freedom* series).

"ALAMO, THE"
J. W. Dant Distillers' 1969 "American Collection of Great Moments in History" bourbon whiskey bottle. This four-fifths quart bottle featured a full-color lithograph of Alamo combatants fighting in the church courtyard.

ALAMO, THE
Leonard Everett Fisher's 1987 publication on the famous siege and battle. The author cited Francisco Antonio Ruiz in describing Crockett's death: "Toward the west, and in the small fort opposite the city, we found the body of Colonel Crockett."

ALAMO, THE
Steve Frazee-authored 1960 historical treatment of the famous battle, published as a promotional paperback to coincide with the release of John Wayne's motion picture, *The Alamo*.

"ALAMO, THE"
Don Gillis' 1947 symphonic poem dedicated to the people of Texas. *The Alamo* was part of a trilogy on symbols of American freedom. The piece was first performed by the San Antonio Symphony Orchestra under the direction of conductor Dr. Max Reiter.

"ALAMO, THE"
Two-hour History Channel cable TV special which initially aired on February 25, 1996. Produced by Arthur Drooker, the program features commentary by Mary Katherine Briggs, Jesus de la Teja, Paul Hutton, Stephen Hardin, Timothy Matovina, Ed Linenthal, Kevin Young, Frank Thompson, Lee Spencer, and Stephen Harrigan.

ALAMO, THE
Thomas J. Kane-edited 1960 promotional premier book of cast photos, action shots and George Phippen drawings which were sold in movie theater lobbies during showings of John Wayne's *The Alamo*.

ALAMO, THE
Walter F. McCaleb's 1956 children's book about the Battle of

the Alamo as told by an old man to his grandson. McCaleb made no mention of Crockett's death, although he noted that Santa Anna probably was taken to see the Tennessean's body after the battle.

"ALAMO, THE"
Monte Enterprises' 1968 cardboard Alamo model kit that included twelve major assembly pieces on sixteen heavy stock sheets.

ALAMO, THE
John Myers Myers' 1948 volume about the Siege and Battle of the Alamo. Of Crockett's death, Myers wrote: "The Tennessean bashed, slashed, smashed, crushed, stamped and rent apart the squads upon squads that came to them. Crockett and two of his men were reported to have been found in a heap with seventeen dead Mexicans."

ALAMO, THE
John Wayne's epic motion picture (1960) about the Siege and Battle of the Alamo. The United Artists film, which was nominated for seven Academy Awards (it won for Best Sound), starred Laurence Harvey (Travis), Richard Widmark (Bowie), and Wayne (Crockett). The film's set, now known as Alamo Village, was subsequently used for several other Alamo films including *Seguin; Houston: The Legend of Texas; The Alamo: 13 Days To Glory;* and *Alamo . . . the Price of Freedom,* among others (see Donald Clark and Christopher Andersen: *John Wayne's The Alamo*).

ALAMO, THE
Columbia Records soundtrack album from John Wayne's *The Alamo.* Dimitri Tiomkin composed and conducted the music on this recording which was released on December 4, 1960, and spent forty-seven weeks on the *Billboard* album charts. This 14-track collection charted as high as #7 (see Joel Whitburn: *Joel Whitburn's Top LP's: 1945-1972*).

ALAMO, THE; AFTER THE FALL
Joseph Musso's 1962 painting which depicted the Alamo church's courtyard following the storming of the Alamo. The

painting was seen on A&E's *Real West* "The Battle of the Alamo" segment in 1992, the History Channel's special on "The Alamo" in 1996, and the *Bowie Knives* video produced by the Butterfield & Butterfield Auction Galleries in 1992.

"ALAMO, THE: A SELECT BIBLIOGRAPHY"

Informative sixteen-page pamphlet listing select bibliographical material available at the Daughters of the Republic of Texas Library at the Alamo. The bibliography was compiled by Linda Edwards and Lisa Zelnick on April 8, 1994, and revised on February 22, 1995.

ALAMO: 1836-1936, THE

Olin W. Archer's Texas centennial book about the famous siege and battle. Of Crockett's death: "But before excited Mexicans could pick off the last of the four, there was one more shot, the last cannon shot fired by the defenders of the Alamo. Crockett's body lay at the west gun station."

"ALAMO, THE: A MEMORIAL TO TEXAN HEROISM"

Ernest William Winkler's 1937 seventeen-page pamphlet about the Shrine of Texas Liberty.

"ALAMO, THE: VICTORY IN DEATH"

Simulations Publications' 1981 war game that featured "one hundred die-cut cardboard playing pieces (with special counters to represent Travis, Crockett, Bowie, and Santa Anna)."

ALAMO AND OTHER POEMS, THE

Viola Berry's 1906 book of poetry. The cover featured a design of an Alamo monument which was erected in Austin, Texas, in 1891 (see Susan Prendergast Schoelwer: *Alamo Images: Changing Perceptions of a Texas Experience*).

ALAMO, THE: ALTAR OF TEXAS LIBERTY

Frederick Charles Chabot's 1931 book about the Shrine of Texas Liberty. Of Crockett's death: "Crockett is reported to have been seen standing calmly, proudly erect with his clubbed rifle in hand dealing death to the foe with an unerring aim."

"ALAMO, THE: AMERICA'S THERMOPYLAE"

The Alamo Monument Association's small sixteen-page pamphlet which coincided with the organization's effort in the late 1870s to build a monument to the Alamo defenders in San Antonio. The undated pamphlet cites Sergeant Becerra's account of Crockett's death: "The two last men killed were Travis and Colonel Crockett. . . ."

"ALAMO, THE: AN IN-DEPTH STUDY OF THE BATTLE"

Author C. D. Huneycutt's flawed 1987 book that includes such undocumented passages as the existence of an Alamo watchtower (with three swivel guns) and Santa Anna's execution of local Tejanos after the March 6, 1836, battle.

ALAMO, THE: CRADLE OF TEXAS LIBERTY

Recently rediscovered unknown Alamo film from the late 1920s (exact date unknown). Only ten stills from the film exist (see "Another Alamo Movie Found" in *The Alamo Journal,* #97, July 1995).

"ALAMO, THE . . . THERMOPYLAE OF TEXAS"

Charles J. Weigel's thirteen-page pamphlet published in 1948 about the famous thirteen-day siege and battle.

ALAMO AND THE TEXAS WAR FOR INDEPENDENCE, THE

Albert Nofi's 1992 book on the Texas Revolution, replete with sidebar descriptions, maps, and photographs. The author compares and contrasts various accounts of Crockett's death. Nofi notes, however, "that the story told by de la Peña is accurate."

"ALAMO AND THE WAR OF TEXAN INDEPENDENCE, 1835-1846, THE"

Philip Haythornthwaite's 1986 booklet in the Osprey military series that features over two dozen color plates of Alamo defenders and Mexican troops.

ALAMO ARTILLERY

Twenty-one artillery pieces (some made of iron, others of brass) were probably at the Alamo during the thirteen-day siege in 1836, according to Thomas R. Lindley of Texian Army

Investigations. Lt. Col. James C. Neill of the Texian Artilley Corps had thirty guns in his force following the Battle of Béxar, twenty of which were acquired from General Cos at the surrender ceremony. Nine guns were taken from Béxar prior to February 23, 1836, the first day of the siege, and sent to such places as Gonzales, Refugio, and Goliad. The Alamo artillery included one nine-inch "Pedrero" (iron), one Spanish sixteen-pounder (iron), one twelve-pound "gunade" (iron), three eight-pounders (two iron, one brass), five six-pounders (brass), four four-pounders (three iron, one brass), two three-pounders (brass), three small pieces of ordnance (two brass, one iron) and the eighteen-pounder (brass), the garrison's largest gun (see Thomas R. Lindley: "Alamo Artillery: Number, Type, Caliber, and Concussion" in *The Alamo Journal*, #82, July 1992).

ALAMO BATTLEFIELD ASSOCIATION
Non-profit historical group formed in 1994. The organization is "dedicated to the preservation and study of the Alamo and the Texas War for Independence."

ALAMO BEACH, TEXAS
Calhoun County settlement located near Port Lavaca on Lavaca Bay.

ALAMO BOWL
First football bowl game played at the newly-constructed Alamodome in San Antonio, Texas on January 21, 1993. The University of California defeated the University of Iowa 37–3.

ALAMO CASUALTIES (MEXICAN)
Several contemporary accounts suggest conflicting casualties (killed and wounded) among the Mexican Army as a result of the March 6, 1836, assault on the Alamo. Col. Juan Almonte noted 288 casualties; Col. Jose Juan Sanchez Navarro: 387; Gen. Santa Anna (official report): 370; Capt. Ruben Potter: 500; Santa Anna (memoirs): 1,000; Felix Nunez: 1,000; Anselmo Borgara: 1,000+; Jesse Badgett: 1,000+; Ben (Travis' slave): 1,200; Ramon Caro: 400-800; Francisco Ruiz: 1,600; and Francisco Becerra: 2,300 (see Edward Dubravsky: "Mexican Losses at the Alamo" in *The Alamo Journal*, #80, February 1992).

ALAMO CASUALTIES (TEXIAN)
Totals for the Alamo defenders range from 189, the current figure identified by the Daughters of the Republic of Texas at the Alamo, to 257, a number stated by Thomas R. Lindley of Texian Army Investigations during an address delivered at the Alamo Society Symposium held at the Menger Hotel in San Antonio, Texas, on March 6, 1993. The figure of 257 coincides with the same number identified by Col. Jose Juan Sanchez Navarro, a Mexican eyewitness (see Albert Nofi: *Alamo and the Texas War for Independence*).

ALAMO CENOTAPH
Erected in 1939 by the Texas Centennial Commission on Alamo Plaza, the monument's Georgia gray marble shaft reaches sixty feet from its pink Texas granite base. Created by Pompeo Coppini, the monument's theme is the "Spirit of Sacrifice," and features Alamo defenders including David Crockett, William B. Travis, James Bowie, and James B. Bonham.

ALAMO CHESS SET
Studio Anne Carlton's custom hand-painted metal chessmen. Inspired by the Texas Sesquicentennial in 1986, this Hull, England-based firm created the handmade pieces that featured William B. Travis as the queen, Jim Bowie as a bishop, and Davy Crockett as a knight. Santa Anna was the other queen. The Lone Star State flag and the national flag of Mexico were represented as the kings on this set which retailed for $485 in 1994.

ALAMO CLASSIC CAR MUSEUM
New Braunfels-located private collection of antique motor vehicles that covers eight decades of automotive technology.

ALAMO CRACKERS
Wild West Products' historical takeoff on "Animal Crackers." Created by Tina Blumenthal in 1993, the Alamo-embellished box contains five different shaped crackers: a ten-gallon hat, a Lone Star, State of Texas, a cowboy boot, and the Alamo church. Packaging script notes: "Remember the Alamo . . . Crackers!" is the cry of a new breed of "snack-

The Alamo Cenotaph, San Antonio, Texas. Leslie W. Bland, photographer. Daughters of the Republic of Texas Library, CN 95.269.

ers. . . ." The most Alamo churches ever found in one box of Alamo Crackers was seven!

ALAMO CREEK
Nineteen-mile-long waterway in Brewster County, Texas. Another shorter waterway, Alamo De Cesario Creek, connects Presidio and Brewster counties.

ALAMO DAGUERREOTYPE
Earliest "photo" image of the Alamo that depicts the church without its signature hump. The 1849 image was located in 1993 and sold at auction by Connecticut rare book dealer William Reese to former Texas governor Dolph Briscoe, who donated it to the University of Texas at Austin's Center for American History. The center displayed it at a 1993 exhibit titled "Images of the Alamo and Related Treasures of the Texas Revolution" (see *Southwestern Historical Quarterly*, Vol. XCVII, No. 3, January 1994).

ALAMO DOCTORS
Five Alamo defenders were physicians: Amos Pollard, William D. Howell, Edward F. Mitchusson, John P. Reynolds, and John W. Thomson (see Pascal Wilkins: "Illness at the Alamo" in *The Alamo Journal*, #85, February 1993).

ALAMODOME
Name given to the $186 million sports structure that debuted the Alamo Bowl on January 31, 1993. The structure features 1.2 million square feet of space that can accommodate 65,000 fans (see *Texas Monthly*, July 1993).

ALAMO FACADES
Inspired architectural creations patterned after the Alamo church's distinctive "hump." Among the twentieth century's most unique Alamo church reproductions were the Alamo Coin Laundry (Willston, FL), the Alamo Plaza Courts Apartments (Little Rock, AK), the Enchanted Forest Alamo (Old Forest, NY), Pioneer Auto Leasing (Plano, TX), Alamo Plaza Hotel Courts (Fort Worth, TX), the Alamo Restaurant (NYC, NY), and the national Lone Star Saloon restaurant

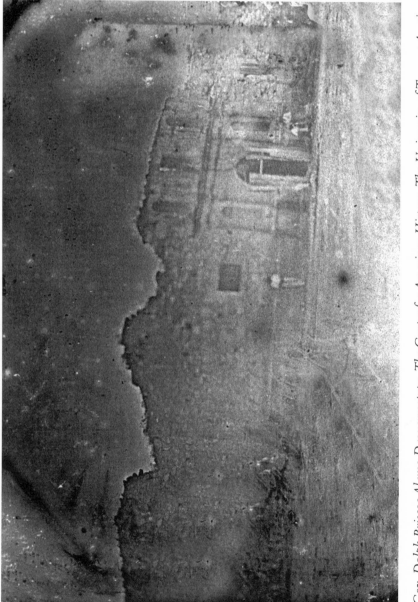

Gov. Dolph Briscoe Alamo Daguerreotype, The Center for American History, The University of Texas at Austin, CN07471

chain, among others (see Susan Prendergast Schoelwer: *Alamo Images: Changing Perceptions of a Texas Experience*).

ALAMO: 8 A.M., THE
Tempera painting by J. Hefter of Santa Anna and his officers viewing the Texian dead in *Texas in Revolt* (1973). A companion piece to *The Alamo: 5 A.M.*

ALAMO: 5 A.M., THE
Tempera painting by J. Hefter of Santa Anna's assault on the Alamo in *Texas in Revolt.* (1973). A companion piece to *The Alamo: 8 A.M.*

ALAMO FARMS WINERY AND VINEYARD
San Antonio-area boutique-style winery that features an underground wine cellar.

ALAMO FLAGS
The only documented Texian flag to fly at the Alamo during the thirteen-day 1836 siege was the First Company of Texan Volunteers flag, the so-called New Orleans Greys banner, which is currently misplaced in a Mexican museum. The 1824 Flag, probably created by Philip Dimmitt, was a Mexican tri-color with 1824 situated in the center white panel. The 1824 flag, which possibly signified allegiance to the Mexican Constitution of 1824, may have flown over the Alamo following the Battle of Béxar in 1835 but it was probably removed for possible use as a standard in the James Grant-directed Matamoros expedition of 1836. A possible Alamo banner could have been a tri-color flag with two stars (one star for Coahuila, the other for Texas) in its center white panel (see Bill and Marjorie K. Walraven: *The Magnificent Barbarians: Little Told Tales of the Texas Revolution*).

ALAMO FOUNDATION
Non-profit organization established in mid-1980s which recommended a long-term educational and architectural plan to restore the modern property around the Alamo to a more 1836 look. The now-defunct group's ideas were later resurrected by a number of individuals in 1994 (see "Alamo Plaza Project Forges Ahead" in *The Alamo Journal*, #57, September 1987).

ALAMO GHOSTS

Spirits who haunt the grounds of the Alamo. Historical ones (anonymous defenders on the walls of the church) and Hollywood ones (John Wayne) have been identified over the years since 1894 (see Rob and Anne Wlodarski: *The Haunted Alamo — A History of the Mission and Guide to Paranormal Activity*).

ALAMO GUARDS

First Regiment ("Alamo Guards") of the Texas Volunteer Guard, organized on October 2, 1885, the fiftieth anniversary of the Gonzales "Come and Take It" incident. The unit was one of twenty-seven volunteer military units that operated in Texas between 1873 and 1887. On July 1, 1993, a new incarnation of the Alamo Guards was reorganized in the Texas State Guard organization with headquarters located in San Antonio (see Valentine J. Belfiglio: *A History of the Texas State Guard*).

"ALAMO HEROES AND THEIR REVOLUTIONARY ANCESTORS, THE"

Genealogical booklet initially published by the Daughters of the American Revolution (Alamo DAR Chapter, O'Shavano DAR Chapter, and the San Antonio de Bexar DAR Chapter) in 1976, largely based on Amelia Williams' *A Critical Study of the Siege of the Alamo and of the Personnel of its Defenders.*

ALAMO HEIGHTS

Bexar County, Texas, area located about five miles northeast of the Alamo. Although the area was originally part of San Antonio in 1836, the citizens of Alamo Heights voted to make it an independent municipality in 1922.

ALAMO IMAGES: CHANGING PERCEPTIONS OF A TEXAS EXPERIENCE

Susan Prendergast Schoelwer's visually comprehensive 1985 volume about the Alamo of history and popular culture. The well-regarded volume coincided with an exhibition of the same name at the DeGolyer Library, Southern Methodist University in Dallas, Texas, from November 16, 1985, to March 14, 1986.

ALAMO, INDIANA
Town in Montgomery County named after the Alamo in Texas.

ALAMO, TEXAS
Town in Hidalgo County named after the Alamo Land and Sugar Company.

ALAMO ALTO, TEXAS
Tiny settlement of some two dozen inhabitants in El Paso County.

ALAMO ARROYO
Twenty-mile-long, steep-sided gulch in Hudspeth County, Texas.

ALAMO INTERNATIONAL
Alamo organization formed by Phil Rosenthal (co-author of *Roll Call at the Alamo*) in 1980. Rosenthal published forty-one newsletters under the titles *Alamo II* (issues #1-25) and *The Alamo News* (issues #26-41) from August 1980 to June 1984. William Chemerka edited issues #42-49 of *The Alamo News* in 1985 and 1986.

"ALAMO JOBE"
Title character played by Kelly Reno in an episode of NBC-TV's *Amazing Stories* in 1985. The episode featured "Alamo Jobe" caught in a time warp between modern San Antonio and the 1836 siege and battle. Steven Spielberg served as executive producer of the series.

ALAMO JOURNAL, THE
The official publication of The Alamo Society. *The Alamo Journal* features articles on both the Alamo of history and the Alamo of popular culture. It began publication in 1986 during the Texas Sesquicentennial. A special double issue, #100, was published in March 1996.

ALAMO LEGACY: ALAMO DESCENDANTS REMEMBER THE ALAMO
Ron Jackson's 1997 book which includes oral accounts of the Mexican participants in the Siege and Battle of the Alamo.

$2.50

February, 1987

THE ALAMO JOURNAL

The Official Newsletter of The Alamo Society

Alamo Journal, February 1987

Jackson utilized hundreds of family interviews to complete this volume which features original drawings by Gary Zaboly.

ALAMO LEGACY AND MISSIONS ASSOCIATION
Living history organization formed in 1995 by Charles Lara, Ricardo Rodriguez, and Dan Cozart to promote Texas and U. S. history through interpretive programs.

ALAMO LORE AND MYTH ORGANIZATION
An Alamo organization formed by Mike Waters, who published sixteen issues of the group's newsletter, *A.L.A.M.O.*, between March 1979 and December 1982. Waters helped organize the Texas Sesquicentennial Alamo battle re-enactment in March 1986 at Alamo Village in Brackettville, Texas, the site where John Wayne filmed *The Alamo*.

ALAMO, THE: MISSION, FORTRESS AND SHRINE
Frederick Charles Chabot's 1936 book about the history of the Shrine of Texas Liberty. Of Crockett's death: "Crockett was shot down in a room of the low barrack, near the gate, where he had taken refuge. His body was found just inside the doorway to the Baptistry."

ALAMO MONUMENTS
Englishman William B. Nangle created the first Alamo monument with stones from the Alamo compound in 1841. The ten-foot-high monument rested in the vestibule of the Texas State Capitol building until a fire severely damaged it in 1881. Its remnants were acquired by the Daughters of the Republic of Texas. A decade later, a new thirty-five-and-a-half-foot Texas granite structure was completed by James Clark and Company of Louisville, Kentucky. However, some of the engraved names on the monument's roster of Alamo defenders are incorrect.

ALAMO MONUMENT ASSOCIATION
Organized on June 3, 1879, and recognized by Texas Secretary of State T. H. Bowman on June 5, 1879, the group set out "to erect an appropriate monument to the heroes of the Alamo who fell fighting for the Independence of the Republic of Texas." The organization planned to hire architect Alfred

Giles, who would design a 165-foot-tall monument. In 1912 Giles proposed his own 802-foot monument, which was never built.

ALAMO MONUMENTAL ASSOCIATION

Advisory and fund-raising group which suggested in 1893 to rebuild the Alamo compound to its 1836 appearance. A century later the Alamo Plaza Study Committee discussed a similar plan. According to the Alamo Monumental Association, work was supposed to begin on the project in February 1894 with unemployed workers. However, the project was never initiated. When commercial interests sold the Alamo to the Daughters of the Republic of Texas in the early twentieth century, the restoration project idea was scrapped for nearly a century (see Frederick C. Chabot: *The Alamo: Mission, Fortress and Shrine*).

ALAMO NICKNAMES

"Cradle of Texas Liberty" and the "Shrine of Texas Liberty" are the two most famous phrases associated with the Alamo. Both phrases appeared in the early twentieth century. The "Shrine of Texas Liberty," for example, appears in the *San Antonio Express* on April 9, 1905. In addition, William McKinley, the first American president to visit the Alamo, referred to the mission-fortress as "this holy spot." In 1908 Adina de Zavala, president of the De Zavala Chapter of the Daughters of the Republic of Texas, referred to the Alamo as "this sacred shrine." Author Frederick C. Chabot wrote a book in 1931 titled *The Alamo: Altar of Texas Liberty*.

ALAMO OAK

The large tree thought to have been growing since 1836 which dominates the Alamo's northern interior courtyard. The tree, however, was planted in 1912 (see *San Antonio Express-News*, July 31, 1994).

ALAMO PLAQUE

Mounted on the front of the Alamo church is a bronze plaque that reads: "Be silent friend, here heroes died to blaze a trail for other men."

ALAMO PLATE

Sesquicentennial "Remember the Alamo" commemorative plate co-sponsored by the Order of Granaderos de Galvez and the William Barret Travis Chapter of the Sons of the Republic of Texas to raise funds in order to "focus on badly needed revitalization projects and educational programs to improve the historical context of the original Alamo compound." The Pickard China firm made 15,000 plates (selling for $150 each) that featured a detail of Robert J. Onderdonk's *The Fall of the Alamo.*

ALAMO PLAYSETS

Miniature plastic and metal toy playsets featuring Alamo defenders and attacking Mexican soldiers. Marx issued several different sets during the Walt Disney Davy Crockett craze in the 1950s. Marx's first set, #3530, was issued with Indians instead of Mexican soldiers. Marx reissued set #3534R in 1995 through Sears stores nationwide and later issued a special #3534R set itself. New York's Toy Soldier Company offered a complete Alamo compound playset and assorted supplementary pieces in 1992. BMC Toys in New Jersey issued an inexpensive "Alamo" playset in 1994, designed by noted Alamo diorama maker Thomas F. Feeley, Jr. In 1996 a highly detailed playset was offered by the Kansas-based Classic Toy Soldiers, Inc.

ALAMO PLAZA

San Antonio Street and corresponding area that is located parallel to the front of the Alamo's Long Barracks. Alamo Plaza, which is now closed to vehicular traffic in front of the Alamo, is the scene for historical re-enactments, ceremonies, parades, and political activity.

ALAMO PLAZA HISTORIC TASK FORCE

Organization chaired by Gary Foreman in the mid-1980s, which attempted to close Alamo Plaza to vehicular traffic and help install historical and educational markers near the Alamo.

ALAMO PLAZA STUDY COMMITTEE

Group chaired by San Antonio councilmen Howard Peak and Roger Perez (established by City Council Ordinance #79745 on March 3, 1994) to study "different options to better define and represent the battle and other periods of history" and "determine the best way to design the closing of Alamo Plaza on a permanent basis." On October 20, 1994, the committee issued a fifty-two-page report which recommended closing Alamo Plaza East to vehicular traffic, preserving all post-1836 buildings in the area, and establishing a visitor center, interpretive history center, and city museum which would highlight all historical phases of the Alamo.

ALAMO . . . THE PRICE OF FREEDOM
George McAlister's 1988 book on the history of Texas which coincided with the release of the IMAX motion picture of the same name. McAlister also co-wrote the screenplay (with director Kieth Merrill) to *Alamo . . . The Price of Freedom* (see Frank Thompson: *Alamo Movies*).

ALAMO . . . THE PRICE OF FREEDOM
Texas Cavalcade Corporation Production, which was filmed at Alamo Village in Brackettville, Texas, during the summer of 1987 and released in the giant-screen IMAX format in March of the following year. The film, which won the Cowboy Hall of Fame's 1988 Wrangler Award for Best Historic Western Film, starred Casey Biggs (Travis), Steve Sandor (Bowie), and Merrill Connally (Crockett) (see Frank Thompson: *Alamo Movies*).

ALAMO RANGERS
Uniformed armed guards hired by the Daughters of the Republic to guard the Alamo and its grounds twenty-four hours a day throughout the year (see Holly Brear: *Inherit the Alamo*).

ALAMO REMEMBERED, THE; TEJANO ACCOUNTS AND PERSPECTIVES
Timothy A. Matovina's 1995 book which explores the "collective legacy of Tejano Alamo accounts." Matovina also clarifies "the dilemma (faced by Tejanos) of choosing sides in the (1835-36) conflict between Mexico and Texas."

ALAMO RENT A CAR
Most well-known of all Alamo-named businesses. Alamo Rent

A Car is the largest independently owned and operated general use car rental company in the United States. In addition, Alamo Rent A Car serves thirty-two other countries. The Fort Lauderdale, Florida-based company serves approximately fifteen million customers and employs more than seven thousand people. In 1995 the company generated $1.39 billion in revenue.

ALAMO RESTAURANT
San Antonio-based restaurants, among others, in the United States. Also the name of a New York City-located eatery with scale-sized Alamo church front entrance way. Located at 304 E. 48th Street, this establishment ("rated #1 by the City of San Antonio, Texas") was the scene of an Alamo Society award presentation to *A Time To Stand* author Walter Lord for the all-time "Favorite Alamo Book" on March 6, 1991.

ALAMO SCOUTS
Allied World War II military unit of ten 10-man reconnaissance teams organized on Fergusson Island off the coast of Australian New Guinea on November 1, 1943, by General Walter Krueger, commanding Alamo Force, United States Army. Krueger, who had served at Fort Sam Houston in San Antonio, Texas, named the unit. The Alamo Scouts lost its designation when it became part of the Sixth Army in September 1944.

ALAMO SOCIETY, THE
An Alamo history organization formed during the Texas Sesquicentennial in 1986 by William Chemerka. The organization's official publication is *The Alamo Journal,* which covers the Alamo of history and popular culture. The Alamo Society sponsors an annual symposium on the Alamo each March 6. The organization received a film credit in the Paramount production *The Naked Gun: From The Files of Police Squad* in 1988 from director David Zucker, an Alamo Society member.

ALAMO SOLDIER: THE STORY OF PEACEFUL MITCHELL
R. L. Templeton's 1976 fictional work about a teenage Alamo

defender. Of Crockett's death: "History records that (Napoleon Bonaparte Mitchell) was one of the thirteen men in Davy Crockett's Tennessee Mounted Volunters who died defending the 'Pallisade' wall of the Alamo."

ALAMO SOLDIERS
Independently published 1989 book written by Phil Rosenthal (co-author of *Roll Call at the Alamo*) which includes an overview of the Battle of the Alamo and biographical sketches of its defenders.

"ALAMO STAR, THE"
Newspaper published in San Antonio by James P. Newcomb in 1854-55. The newspaper was the first commercial enterprise to exploit the Alamo's name. The Witte Museum in San Antonio, Texas, published a four-page tabloid titled *The Alamo Star* to coincide with its sesquicentennial exhibition in 1986, "Remembering the Alamo: The Development of a Texas Symbol, 1836-1936."

ALAMO POSTAGE STAMPS
U.S. postage stamps that featured the Alamo include the March 2, 1936 (first day of issue) Texas Centennial 3-cent and a June 14, 1956 (first day of issue) 9-cent.

"ALAMO: 13 DAYS TO GLORY"
Television movie (1987) based upon the 1958 Lon Tinkle book, *13 Days To Glory*. This production was filmed at Alamo Village in Brackettville, Texas, and utilized stock battle footage from *The Last Command*. Directed by Burt Kennedy and starring Alec Baldwin (Travis), James Arness (Bowie), and Brian Keith (Crockett), this TV movie was voted "Worst Alamo Film" of all time by The Alamo Society in a 1989 poll (see Frank Thompson: *Alamo Movies*).

ALAMO VILLAGE
Section of the late James T. "Happy" Shahan's West Texas ranch in Brackettville that has served as a movie set since John Wayne's Batjac Production *The Alamo* was filmed there in 1959. A number of motion pictures were filmed in the area prior to 1959, but Alamo Village remains inextricably linked with

Wayne's epic release. Other Alamo-related films shot there include *Seguin; Houston: The Legend of Texas; The Alamo: 13 Days To Glory; Alamo . . . The Price of Freedom;* and *James Michener's "Texas"* (see Frank Thompson: *Alamo Movies*).

ALL THE BRAVE RIFLES
Clarke Venable's 1929 fictional work about the famous thirteen-day Alamo siege. The author included a historic footnote describing Crockett's death: "It is enough to know that every man died at his post and that their death lifted Texas from its apathy and lighted the beacon of liberty and independence."

ALLEN, JAMES
Kentucky-born Alamo courier, 21, who was probably the last man to leave the mission-fortress before the final assault of March 6, 1836 (see Walter Lord: *A Time To Stand*).

ALLEN, ROBERT
Virginia-born Alamo defender of unknown age who died in the March 6 assault (see Daughters of the Republic of Texas: *The Alamo Long Barrack Museum*).

ALLEY, THOMAS
Texian infantry company commander in Col. Francis W. Johnson's Second Division during the Siege and Battle of Béxar in 1835 (see Alwyn Barr: *Texans in Revolt*).

ALDAMA BATTALION
First Brigade infantry unit under Col. Antonio Goana assigned, in part, to Gen. Martin Perfecto de Cos' assault column of March 6, 1836 (see Stephen L. Hardin: *Texian Iliad*).

ALMONTE, JUAN
Military aid (colonel) to Santa Anna during the Texas Revolution who survived San Jacinto (see Albert Nofi: *The Alamo and the Texas War for Independence*).

ALSBURY, JUANA NAVARRO PEREZ
Tejano noncombatant and wife of Dr. Horace Alsbury, a veteran of the Battle of Béxar. Juana and her sister, Gertrudis Navarro, were eyewitnesses to fighting in the Alamo church

during the March 6 assault. She died on July 23, 1888 (see Crystal Sasse Ragsdale: *Women and Children of the Alamo*).

ALTER, ROBERT EDMOND
Author of the children's book, *Two Sieges of the Alamo.*

AMAT, AUGUSTIN
Mexican colonel under Santa Anna who commanded nearly four hundred elite infantry reserves (primarily men of the Zapadores Battalion and grenadores from other units) against the Alamo on March 6, 1836 (see Albert Nofi: *The Alamo and the Texas War for Independence*).

"AMAZING STORIES"
NBC-TV series which featured a 1985 episode, "Alamo Jobe," about a youngster caught in an Alamo time warp.

ANAHUAC
East Texas town and site of a military showdown between Mexican officials and several dozen anti-tax Texians under William Barret Travis on June 29, 1835. The next day the Mexican garrison under Capt. Antonio Tenorio surrendered its arms to Travis. Anahuac had been the scene of anti-Mexican economic policy disturbances in 1832 (see Paul D. Lack: *The Texas Revolutionary Experience*).

ANDERSON, A.
Assistant quartermaster of the Alamo who died in the March 6 assault, but is currently not acknowledged as a defender (see Thomas R. Lindley: "A Correct List of Alamo Patriots" in *The Alamo Journal*, #89, Dec. 1993).

ANDROSS, MILES DEFOREST
Vermont-born Alamo defender, 27, (real name was Mills Andrews) who died in the March 6, 1836, battle (see Thomas R. Lindley: "A Correct List of Alamo Patriots" in *The Alamo Journal*, #89, December 1993).

ARCHER, OLIN W.
Author of the 1936 publication *The Alamo: 1836-1936.*

ARMSTRONG, ROBERT
Character actor who played David Crockett in *Man of Con-*

quest (1939). He is best known for his role as "Carl Denham," the captor of *King Kong* (see Frank Thompson: *Alamo Movies*).

ARNESS, JAMES
Actor best known for his character "Matt Dillon" on TV's *Gunsmoke* who played Jim Bowie in *The Alamo: 13 Days To Glory* (1987) (see Frank Thompson: *Alamo Movies*).

AROCHA, MACEDONIO
Member of Juan Seguin's cavalry company (see Paul D. Lack: *The Texas Revolutionary Experience*).

ARPA, JOSE
Painter who created *The Funeral Pyre*, which depicts the distant burning of the Alamo defenders in the area behind the Long Barracks. The painting was featured on the cover of Virgil E. Baugh's *Rendezvous at the Alamo*, a Bison Books 1985 reprint.

AT THE BATTLE OF THE ALAMO
One of the titles in the children's "We Were There" historical book series. Written by Margaret Cousins, this 1958 volume traces the Alamo experiences of a fictitious boy who survives the March 6 battle.

AUSTIN, MOSES
Connecticut-born *empressario* of Texas. The historical marker in front of his birth house on Main Stret in Durham, Connecticut, reads: "Here was born, 1761 Moses Austin whose plan led to settlement of Texas by his son Stephen."

AUSTIN, STEPHEN
Virginia-born *empressario* who helped develop the American colonies in Texas during the early 1820s. Fulfulling the wishes of his father, Moses, who arranged with Spain the right to colonize Texas prior to Mexican independence in 1821, Austin established the "Old Three Hundred," the first 297 families to settle the lands around the settlement of San Felipe de Austin. Austin became the spokesman for the developing Anglo influence in Texas and was later imprisoned for eighteen months

by the Mexican government for suggesting that the citizens of San Antonio de Béxar initiate steps toward statehood. Following his release from prison, Austin argued strongly for independence on September 8, 1835, during a speech in Brazoria. On October 18, 1835, he was elected to command the embryonic Texian army; however, he was relieved of that position a month later. He served as the Republic of Texas' first secretary of state in 1836 (see Eugene C. Barker: "Stephen F. Austin and the Independence of Texas" in *Quarterly of the Texas State Historical Association,* #13, April 1910).

AUSTIN, MRS. STEPHEN F.
Author of the 1936 publication *The Alamo.*

**"AUTHENTIC ALAMO ACTION FIGURES
 AND PLAYSET"**
BMC Toys' 1994 plastic playset of 54mm figures created by Thomas F. Feely, Jr., the diorama artist who made "Crockett's Last Stand" for the Texas Adventure™ in San Antonio. The playset box art featuring Crockett, Bowie, and Travis was based on an original work created by artist Michael Boldt.

AUTRY, MICAJAH
North Carolina-born Alamo defender, 42, who arrived in San Antonio with David Crockett in early February 1836. Autry died in the March 6 assault (see Richard Crawford: "A Man Called Micajah" in *The Alamo Journal,* June 1990).

AVALON, FRANKIE
Pop singing idol who played "Smitty" in John Wayne's *The Alamo* and released *Frankie Avalon as "Smitty" Sings Songs of "The Alamo"* in 1960. Avalon's Chancellor Records extended-play recording was joined by eighteen other Alamo-related 45 rpm singles releases from various artists in 1960-61 (see Donald Clark and Christopher Andersen: *John Wayne's The Alamo*).

BABER, RALPH K.
Texas author of the Alamo play *The Silenced Cannon* and *From the Alamo Front and De La Frente Alamo,* a fictional ac-

count of the Battle of the Alamo "reported" by Texian B. K. Rolfe and Mexican Rafael Baber.

BABBITT, E. B.
United States Army major and quartermaster in San Antonio who supervised the construction of the Alamo in 1850. An earlier reconstruction plan under the supervision of Captain R. A. Alston in 1847 was never implemented. The mechanics under Babbitt's authority built a roof and crafted the identifiable parapet that graces the top of the church today. A Bavarian immigrant, however, named John M. Fries, may have been responsible for influencing the distinguishable shape of the arch (see Jim Steeley: "Remembering the Alamo" in *Texas Highways*, March 1985).

BACHILLER, CAPT. MIGUEL
Mexican courier who was captured by Erastus "Deaf" Smith on April 18, 1836. Bachiller was carrying communications from Santa Anna to General Filisola in Travis' saddlebags (see Albert Nofi: *The Alamo and the Texas War for Independence*).

BADILLO, JUAN ANTONIO
Tejano veteran of the Battle of Bexar and a member of Juan Seguin's cavalry who died at the Alamo (see Bill Groneman: *Alamo Defenders*).

BAILEY, PETER JAMES
Kentucky-born Alamo defender, 24, who died in March 6 assault (see Daughters of the Republic of Texas: *The Alamo Long Barrack Museum*).

BAKER RIFLE
Surplus British rifle, .625 caliber, which was used by some of Santa Anna's troops during the Texas Revolution. The Baker rifle, named for London gunmaker Ezekiel Baker, initially utilized a 23-inch sword bayonet. Baker is reported to have hit a man-sized target thirty-two out of thirty-four times at one hundred yards with his creation. Most Mexican infantry, however, used surplus British "Brown Bess" muskets (see Ed Dubravsky: "The Baker Rifle" in *The Alamo Journal*, #93, October 1994).

BAKER, ISAAC G.
Arkansas territory-born member, 32, of the Gonzales Ranging Company who died at the Alamo (see Bill Groneman: *Alamo Defenders*).

BAKER, MOSELY
Company commander in Sam Houston's army who skirmished with Santa Anna at San Felipe in early April. Baker was critical of Houston's decision not to engage his men against Santa Anna in the weeks following the exodus from Gonzales. Baker took part in the Battle of San Jacinto (see Stephen L. Hardin: *Texian Iliad*).

BAKER, WILLIAM CHARLES
Missouri-born Alamo officer of unknown age who died in the March 6 assault (see Bill Groneman: *Alamo Defenders*).

"BALLAD OF THE ALAMO"
Marty Robbins' 1960 Columbia Records hit single, from *The Alamo* soundtrack LP, which spent five weeks on the charts. The tune, which is also included on *More Greatest Hits: Marty Robbins*, reached the #34 position (see Joel Whitburn: *The Billboard Book of Top 40 Hits*).

"BALLAD OF DAVY CROCKETT"
Popular tune written by Tom Blackburn (lyrics) and George Bruns (music) that accompanied Walt Disney's *Davy Crockett, King of the Wild Frontier* on TV during 1954-55 season. The twenty-verse song, which contained a verse about the Alamo, was recorded by nearly twenty artists in 1955, including Tommy Scott, Gabe Drake and the Woodsman, Bill Hart and the Mountaineers, and the Sandpipers, among others. Four of the versions were Top 40 hits: Walter Schumann reached #14; "Tennessee" Ernie Ford hit #5; Fess Parker, who played Davy Crockett in the TV show, also reached #5; and Bill Hayes topped the charts for five weeks (see Joel Whitburn: *The Billboard Book of Top 40 Hits*).

BALDWIN, ALEC
Actor who played William Barret Travis in *The Alamo: 13 Days To Glory* (see Frank Thompson: *Alamo Movies*).

BALLENTINE, JOHN J.
Pennsylvania-born artillerist of unknown age (real name: James T. Vallentine) who died at the Alamo (see Thomas R. Lindley: "A Correct List of Alamo Patriots" in *The Alamo Journal*, #89, December 1993).

BALLENTINE, RICHARD W.
Scotsman, 22, who died at the Alamo (see Daughters of the Republic of Texas: *The Alamo Long Barrack Museum*).

BARCENAS, ANDRES
Tejano rancher who, along with Anselmo Bargaras, informed Houston's army at Gonzales on March 11 that the Alamo had fallen. Houston arrested them as being Santa Anna's men, although he believed them. Their story was validated two days later by Susanna Dickinson (see Albert Nofi: *The Alamo and the War for Texas Independence*).

BARKER, EUGENE C.
Well-regarded historian and past president of the Texas State Historical Association. Barker authored a number of important books and articles on the Alamo and the Texas Revolution, including *Mexico and Texas, 1821-1835* in 1928, *The Austin Papers* in 1919, *Readings in Texas History* in 1929, and "The Texas Revolutionary Army," in the April 1906 edition of the *Quarterly of the Texas State Historical Association.*

BARGARAS, ANSELMO
Member of Juan Seguin's cavalry company who accompanied Andres Barcenas to Gonzales on March 11, 1836, in order to alert the settlement of the Alamo's fate. Bargaras and Barcenas were arrested by Houston, although he believed their story. Their account was validated by Susanna Dickinson on March 13 (see Albert Nofi: *The Alamo and the War for Texas Independence*).

BARR, ALWYN
Texas Tech University-based author of *Texans in Revolt*, a 1990 book about the Siege and Battle of Béxar in 1835.

BARR, AMELIA E.
Author of the 1888 fictional work *Remember the Alamo*.

BARRATT, ROBERT
Veteran character actor who played David Crockett in *Man of Conquest* (1939) (see Frank Thompson: *Alamo Movies*).

BARRETT, MONTE
Author of 1946 fictional novel, *The Tempered Blade*, about the life of Jim Bowie. The book's cover art features Bowie, armed with what looks like a World War II bayonet, fighting a Mexican soldier in front of an anachronistic Alamo church.

BARTON, WILLIAM
Creator of poem "Texas Song of Liberty" which appeared in the book *Heroes of the Alamo* (1956). The poem begins: "When the locusts of tyranny darkened our land/And our friends were reduced to a small Spartan band/When the Alamo reeked with the blood of the brave/And Mexican faith slept in Goliad's grave."

BATTALION DE TRES VILLAS
Mexican infantry battalion recruited from the villages of Cordoba, Jalapa, and Orizaba, and commanded by Col. Don Cayatono Montoya in Bvt. Gen. Jose Urrea's Division during coastal operations in February and March 1836. The unit participated in the Battle of Coleto and the execution of Fannin's men at Goliad on March 27, 1836 (see Stephen L. Hardin: *Texian Ilaid*).

BATTISTA, LLOYD
Actor who played Santa Anna in the 1995 TV movie *James A. Michener's "Texas."*

BATTLE OF THE ALAMO
Keith Murphy's 1979 children's book (illustrations by Trevor Parkin) is essentially a condensed Davy Crockett biography. Of Crockett's death: "Near where Crockett fell, lay the bodies of seventeen dead Mexican soldiers."

"BATTLE OF THE ALAMO, THE"
Ben. H. Procter's 1986 booklet on the Siege and Battle of Bexar the Alamo's thirteen-day siege. *The Battle of the Alamo* was published by the Texas Historical Commission to coincide with the Texas Sesquicentennial.

"BATTLE OF THE ALAMO, THE"
Hour-long segment of the Arts & Entertainment (A&E) cable TV network's *Real West* series, which initially aired on September 24, 1992. Hosted by Kenny Rogers, the program featured commentary from Walter Lord, Paul Hutton, Stephen Hardin, Kevin Young, Joe Musso, Gilberto Hinojosa, and William Chemerka.

"BATTLE OF THE ALAMO"
Hour-long Discovery Channel cable TV special which initially aired on March 3, 1996. Hal Holbrook narrated the Paul Wagner-directed effort which traced each of the thirteen days of the Alamo siege. Two recreated scenes were actually filmed inside the sacristy of the Alamo.

BATTLES OF TEXAS
Joe B. Frantz authored "The Alamo" chapter of this 1967 chronological anthology which featured the artwork of Donald M. Yena.

BAUGH, CAPT. JOHN J.
Virginia-born adjutant of the Alamo, 33, who died in the March 6 assault (see Stephen L. Hardin: *Texian Iliad*).

BAUGH, VIRGIL
Author of *Rendezvous at the Alamo: Highlights in the Lives of Bowie, Crockett, and Travis* (1960). The author offers no description of Crockett's death.

BAYLISS, JOSEPH
Tennessee-born defender, 28, who died at the Alamo (see Daughters of the Republic of Texas: *The Alamo Long Barrack Museum*).

BAYLOR, JOHN WALKER, JR.
Kentucky-born Alamo courier, 22, who was wounded in the thigh during the Battle of San Jacinto. His wound never properly healed, and Baylor died on September 3, 1836 (see Bill Groneman: *Alamo Defenders*).

BECERRA, FRANCISCO
First sergeant in Santa Anna's army and combatant at Alamo

and San Jacinto. Becerra's personal account of the Alamo (the San Jacinto entries have been lost) delivered to former Texas Ranger John S. "Rip" Ford in 1875 can be found in *A Mexican Sergeant's Recollections of the Alamo & San Jacinto.* Becerra's reminiscences are somewhat suspect, however, since he claims to have been present at the deaths of Travis, Bowie, and Crockett.

BENAVIDES, PLACIDO
Tejano commander of infantry company in Col. Francis W, Johnson's Second Division during Siege and Battle of Béxar in 1835 (see Alwyn Barr: *Texans in Revolt*).

BENECKE, TEX
Orchestra leader who released *Music From The Film The Alamo* on RCA in 1960 (see Donald Clark and Christopher Andersen: *John Wayne's The Alamo*).

BEN HARDIN'S CROCKETT ALMANAC OF 1842
Publication which featured the first illustration of Crockett battling at the Alamo. An unknown artist depicted Crockett with the caption "Crockett's Fight With The Mexicans." The almanac also promoted the idea that Crockett had been captured at the Alamo and sent to Mexico to work in the mines (see Susan Prendergast Schoelwer: *Alamo Images: Changing Perceptions of a Texas Experience*).

BENNETT, LEONORA
Author of 1904 publication, *Historical Sketch and Guide to the Alamo.*

BERRY, VIOLA
Author of 1906 book, *The Alamo and Other Poems.*

BEXAR
Abbreviated name for San Antonio de Béxar. The town also provided men in one of seven Mexican cavalry companies stationed at the Alamo in 1835 (see Alwyn Barr: *Texans in Revolt: The Battle For San Antonio, 1835*).

BIGGS, CASEY
Actor who played William Barret Travis in *Alamo . . . The Price of Freedom* (see Frank Thompson: *Alamo Movies*).

BINKLEY, WILLIAM C.
Vanderbilt University history department chairman and author of 1952 book *The Texas Revolution,* a compilation of four Louisiana State University lectures.

BIRTH OF TEXAS
Subtitle to 1915 film, *The Martyrs of the Alamo* (see Frank Thompson: *Alamo Movies*).

BISSETT, WILLIAM
Scotsman who worked as a chain carrier for a San Antonio surveying firm in 1838 and painted *The Alamo,* an 1839 watercolor. The painting was later copied by Ida Johns, the twelve-year-old granddaughter of I. A. Clark, who had been given *The Alamo* by Bissett (see Craig Covner: "Before 1850: A New Look at the Alamo Through Art and Imagery" in *The Alamo Journal, #73,* November 1990).

BLAIR, JOHN
Tennessee-born Alamo defender, 33, who died in the March 6 assault (see Walter Lord: *A Time To Stand*).

BLAIR, SAMUEL
Tennesse-born Alamo officer (captain) and ordnance chief, 29, who died in March 6 assault (see Phil Rosenthal and Bill Groneman: *Roll Call at the Alamo*).

BLAKE, JACOB EDMUND
U.S. Army lieutenant who drew the ink rendition, *Ruins of the Alamo,* in 1845 (see Craig Covner: "Before 1850: A New Look at the Alamo Through Art and Imagery" in *The Alamo Journal, #73,* November 1990).

BLAZING DAWN, THE
James Wakefield Burke's 1975 "tempestuous saga of the Alamo" that features risque David Crockett love scenes. Of Crockett's death: "David's right arm is blown off, his companions killed instantly. Trailing blood and strings of pulverized flesh and bone, David steps into the clearing of the hallway. Yelling fiercely, he cries 'I'm still here! Come and get me!' A hail of gunfire cuts him down."

BOLLAERT, WILLIAM
English traveller to San Antonio who drew a sketch of the Alamo in 1843 from the Veramendi house (see Craig Covner: "Before 1850: A New Look at the Alamo Through Art and Imagery" in *The Alamo Journal*, #70, March 1990).

BONHAM, JAMES BUTLER
South Carolina-born Alamo officer (second lieutenant) and courier, 29. Bonham returned to the mission-fortress on March 3 with several dispatches, including an encouraging one from Maj. Robert M. ("Three-Legged Willie") Williamson who instructed Travis to hold on until help came from various Texian settlements. Bonham died in the March 6 assault (see Thomas Ricks Lindley: "James Butler Bonham" in *The Alamo Journal*, August 1988).

BOWIE, JAMES
Kentucky-born Alamo officer (colonel), 40, who moved to Texas in 1828 with the reputation as a famous knife-fighter (thanks, in part, to the knife made by his brother, Rezin). Bowie participated in the Battle of Béxar, was elected commander of the volunteers on February 12, 1836, and shared command of the Alamo with Travis on February 14. An unspecified illness forced him to yield his leadership position during the early days of the Alamo siege. Bowie died in his quarters during the March 6 assault (see Raymond W. Thorp: *Bowie Knife*).

BOWIE KNIFE
Any large hunting knife/butcher knife, but specifically the long-bladed knife carried by Jim Bowie, who popularized the weapon at the Sandbar Fight near Natchez, Mississippi, in 1827. According to Bowie Knife authority Joseph Musso, Bowie used several different knives in his lifetime. Bowie's brother, Rezin, and knifemaker James Black made knives for Bowie, but it is not known with certainty what kind of knife Bowie possessed during the Siege and Battle of the Alamo (see Joe Musso: "A Bowie Knife" in *The Alamo Journal*, #84, December 1992).

"BIG JIM"
BOWIE,
GENTLEMAN
FROM THE
BAYOU.

"Big Jim Bowie, Gentleman From the Bayou." Illustration by Gary Zaboly

BOWMAN, JESSE B.

Alleged Alamo defender; however, the headright land grants to him do not identify Bowman serving in the military (see Thomas R. Lindley: "A Correct List of Alamo Patriots" in *The Alamo Journal,* #89, December 1993).

BREAR, HOLLY

Virginia-based author of *Inherit the Alamo* (1995), an anthropological study of the Alamo and the sociological groups that relate to it.

BREECE, THOMAS H.

Texian infantry company commander in Col. Francis W. Johnson's Second Division during Siege and Battle of Béxar in 1835 (see Alwyn Barr: *Texans in Revolt*).

BROGAN, EVELYN

Author of the 1922 book *James Bowie: A Hero of the Alamo.*

BROWN BESS

Nickname given to British-made .75 caliber, flintlock smoothbore musket which was the basic infantryman's shoulder weapon from early eighteenth to early nineteenth century. Several models evolved during its history, including the India Pattern, which was developed in 1793 and later sold as surplus to Mexico. Many of Santa Anna's soldiers were equipped with the Brown Bess during the invasion of Texas in 1836 (see William Chemerka: "The Brown Bess Musket of Santa Anna's Army" in *The Alamo News,* #44, April 1985).

BROWN, GEORGE

Englishman, 35, who died at the Alamo (see Daughters of the Republic of Texas: *The Alamo Long Barrack Museum*).

BROWN, JAMES

Pennsylvania-born Alamo defender, 36, who died in the March 6 assault (see Daughters of the Republic of Texas: *The Alamo Long Barrack Museum*).

BROWN, ROBERT

Alamo courier, 18, who left the mission-fortress after February 25, 1836 (see Bill Groneman: *Alamo Defenders*).

BUCHANAN, JAMES
Alabama-born Alamo defender, 23, who died in March 6, 1836, assault (see Daughters of the Republic of Texas: *The Alamo Long Barrack Museum*).

BUGLES ARE SILENT, THE
John R. Knaggs' 1977 historical novel about the Alamo.

"BUILD THE ALAMO"
Title of Mark Wheatley's 1982 cardboard cutout construction booklet that allows one to build a modern Alamo church.

BURKE, JAMES WAKEFIELD BURKE
Author of the 1975 historical novel about the Alamo, *The Blazing Dawn.*

BURLESON, COL. EDWARD
Commander of the "First Texas Volunteer regiment." Sam Houston appointed Burleson to the position (with Lt. Col. Sidney Sherman as second-in-command) on March 12, the day after Andres Barcenas and Anselmo Bargaras notified Gonzales that the Alamo had fallen (see Albert Nofi: *The Alamo and the War for Texas Independence*).

BURNET, DAVID GOUVERNEUR
Newark, New Jersey-born *empressario* who was elected the Republic of Texas' first chief executive by the General Convention. Burnet served as president *ad interim* of Texas from March 17 to October 22, 1836. Lorenzo de Zavala served as his vice president (see Mary Whatley Clarke: *David G. Burnet*).

BURNET, HANNAH ESTE
Morristown, New Jersey-born wife of David G. Burnet, first president of the Republic of Texas. Burnet was born on December 8, 1800, and died in 1858. Her gravestone in Baytown, now lost, incorrectly stated her husband's term as president starting one day too early on March 16, 1836 (see Mary Whatley Clarke: *David G. Burnet*).

BURNS, SAMUEL E.
Irish artillerist, 26, who died at the Alamo (see Bill Groneman: *Alamo Defenders*).

BUSCHBACHER, FRANK
Texas-based archaeologist who conducted an unsuccessful Alamo dig in February and March 1995 to find a hidden nineteenth century well containing Jim Bowie's alleged San Saba treasure.

BUTLER, GEORGE D.
Missouri-born Alamo defender, 23, who was killed in March 6 assault (see Daughters of the Republic of Texas: *The Alamo Long Barrack Museum*).

BUTTERFIELD, J. C.
Author of 1913 pamphlet, "The Story of the Alamo." Of Crockett's death: "The Texans club their guns; one by one they fall fighting — now Travis yonder by the western wall, now Crockett here in the angle of the church wall . . ."

CAIN, JOHN
Pennsylvania-born artillerist, 34, who was killed at the Alamo (see Bill Groneman: *Alamo Defenders*).

CAMPBELL, ROBERT
Tennessee-born Alamo officer (lieutenant), 26, who was killed at the Alamo (see Bill Groneman: *Alamo Defenders*).

CANNON BOY OF THE ALAMO
R. L. Templeton's 1975 children's book about the Alamo's youngest defender. "Read Billy King's story. Feel what it was like to die at age 15 in the Alamo, beside Crockett, Bowie, Travis, and grizzled old cannoneer Sergeant William Ward," noted the book's promotional text.

CAREY, WILLIAM R.
Virginia-born Alamo gunner, 30, who commanded the Alamo's artillery. Carey was killed in the March 6 battle (see Walter Lord: *A Time To Stand*).

CARLSON, RICHARD
Actor who played William Barret Travis in *The Last Command* (1955) (see Frank Thompson: *Alamo Movies*).

CARO, D. RAMON MARTINEZ
Santa Anna's secretary who commented on the Battle of the

Alamo in *The Mexican Side of the Texan Revolution.* Noted Caro: "Among the 183 killed there were five who were discovered by General Castrillon after the assault. He took them immediately to his Excellency who had come up by this time. When he presented the prisoners he was severely reprimanded for not having killed them on the spot, after which he turned his back upon Castrillon while the soldiers stepped out of their ranks and set upon the prisoners until they were all killed."

CARTER, ALDEN C.
Wisconsin-based author of *Last Stand at the Alamo,* a 1990 children's book.

CASTENEDA, CARLOS E.
Translator of *The Mexican Side of the Texan Revolution,* which includes information supplied by Generals Santa Anna, Filisola, Urrea, and Tornel, plus D. Ramon Martinez Caro, Santa Anna's secretary. Of the attack on the Alamo, Santa Anna noted: "Let us weep at the tomb of the brave Mexicans who died at the Alamo defending the honor and the rights of their country."

CASTRILLON, MANUEL FERNANDEZ
Mexican brigadier general who brought the handful of captured Alamo defenders to Santa Anna following the March 6, 1836, battle. Castrillon hoped they would be spared, but Santa Anna criticized him for not immmediatey killing them. Castrillon was killed at the Battle of San Jacinto (see Carlos E. Castaneda, trans.: *The Mexican Side of the Texas Revolution*).

CAZADORES COMPANY
Mexican light infantry company in Santa Anna's army during the Texas Revolution. The *cazadores* company was one of eight infantry companies within a regiment.

CHABOT, FREDERICK CHARLES
Author of the 1931 book, *The Alamo: Altar of Texas Liberty* and the 1935 publication, *The Alamo: Mission, Fortress and Shrine.*

CHARLI, PEDRO
Earliest known recipient of Alamo property. Charli received the southwest corner room of the compound in 1785.

CHIDSEY, DONALD BARR
Connecticut-based author who wrote the 1961 children's booklet, "The Fall of the Alamo."

CLAIBORNE, ARIE M.
Author of 1904 publication, *The Story of the Alamo.*

CLARK, CHARLES HENRY
Missouri-born Alamo defender of unknown age who was killed in the March 6, 1836, battle (see Daughters of the Republic of Texas: *The Alamo Long Barrack Museum*).

CLARK, M. B.
Mississippi-born Alamo defender of unknown age who was killed in the March 6, 1836, battle (see Daughters of the Republic of Texas: *The Alamo Long Barrack Museum*).

CLASSIC TOY SOLDIERS' THE LEGEND OF THE ALAMO! PLAYSET
Highly detailed Alamo compound playset produced by David Payne's Kansas-based Classic Toy Soldiers, Inc. in 1996. The playset features box art by Craig Covner and includes a booklet, "The Legend of the Alamo," written by Frank Thompson, author of *Alamo Movies.*

COCHRAN, ROBERT E.
New Jersey-born Alamo artillerist, 26, who was killed in the March 6, 1836, battle (see Daughters of the Republic of Texas: *The Alamo Long Barrack Museum*).

COMPANY "G"
Second United States Cavalry company that was the first United States unit to occupy the Alamo, on October 28, 1845.

CONDELLE, NICHOLAS
Mexican officer (colonel) who commanded the highly regarded Morelos Battalion in the 1835 Siege and Battle of Béxar (see Alwyn Barr: *Texas in Revolt*).

CONNALLY, MERRILL
Actor who played David Crockett in 1988 IMAX film *Alamo . . . The Price of Freedom* (see Frank Thompson: *Alamo Movies*).

COOKE, WILLIAM G.
Texian infantry company commander in Col. Francis W. Johnson's Second Division during Siege and Battle of Béxar (see Alwyn Barr: *Texans in Revolt*).

COTTLE, GEORGE WASHINGTON
Missouri-born member of Gonzales Ranging Company, 25, who fought in skirmish for Gonzales cannon on October 2, 1835. Cottle's brother-in-law, Thomas J. Jackson, was also a member of Alamo garrison. Both were killed in the March 6, 1836 battle (see Bill Groneman: *Alamo Defenders*).

COURTMAN, HENRY
German Alamo defender, 28, who was killed in the March 6 1836, battle (see Daughters of the Republic of Texas: *The Alamo Long Barrack Museum*).

"CRADLE OF TEXAS LIBERTY"
One of two major reverent nicknames associated with the Alamo. "The Shrine of Texas Liberty" is the other.

CRANE, JOHN
Texian infantry captain in Ben Milam's division during Siege and Battle of Béxar in 1835 (see Alwyn Barr: *Texans in Revolt*).

CRAWFORD, LEMUEL
South Carolina-born artillerist, 22, who was killed in the March 6, 1836, Battle of the Alamo (see Daughters of the Republic of Texas: *The Alamo Long Barrack Museum*).

CRISP, JAMES E.
Associate professor of history at North Carolina State University who has written about the Alamo for a number of historical publications in the 1990s. Dr. Crisp discounts the idea that the Jose Enrique de la Peña account of the Battle of the Alamo is a forgery (see James Crisp: "The Little Book That Wasn't There: The Myth and Mystery of the de la Peña Diary" in the October 1994 issue of the *Southwestern Historical Quarterly*.)

CROCKETT, DAVID
Famous Tennessean, 49, who traveled to Texas following his

defeat in the House of Representatives election of 1835. Crockett, who served in the Creek Indian War (1813-1814), was sworn into Capt. William Harrison's company in the Volunteer Auxilliary Corps of Texas at Nacogdoches on January 14, 1836. Crockett served as a private during the thirteen-day siege of the Alamo. In a letter dated February 25, Travis extolled Crockett as being "seen at all points, animating the men to do their duty." Crockett was killed during the March 6 assault. However, a modern debate continues about how Crockett died (see Gary Foreman: *Gentleman From The Cane*).

CROCKETT, M. H.
Co-editor (with A. Garland Adair) of the 1956 book *Heroes of the Alamo*.

CROSSMAN, ROBERT
Pennsylvania-born Alamo defender, 26, who was killed in the March 6, 1836, battle (see Daughters of the Republic of Texas: *The Alamo Long Barrack Museum*).

CRUZ Y AROCHA, ANTONIO
Tejano Alamo courier of unknown age who left the mission-fortress with Juan Seguin on February 25, 1836. He later participated in the Battle of San Jacinto (see Bill Groneman: *Alamo Defenders*).

CUELLER, JESUS "COMANCHE"
Ex-Mexican officer who left General Cos' command to join Texian forces in Béxar, his home. Cueller's time spent as a captive with the ubiquitous Comanches of Texas resulted in his nickname (see Stephen L. Hardin: *Texian Iliad*).

CUMMINGS, DAVID P.
Pennsylvania-born Alamo defender, 27, who was killed in the March 6, 1836, battle (see Daughters of the Republic of Texas: *The Alamo Long Barrack Museum*).

CUNNINGHAM, ROBERT
New York-born artillerist, 31, who was killed at the Alamo (see Walter Lord: *A Time To Stand*).

Crockett's arrival on the outskirts of Bexar. Illustration by Gary Zaboly.

DARST, JACOB
Kentucky-born member of Gonzales Ranging Company, 42, who was killed at the Alamo (see Mary Ann Noonan Guerra: *Heroes of the Alamo and Goliad*).

DAUGHTERS OF THE REPUBLIC OF TEXAS (DRT)
Organization established in 1891 dedicated "to perpetuate the memory and spirit of the men and women who have achieved and maintained the independence of Texas." President general is the highest elected office in the organization. The DRT also encourages historical research and celebrates key events of the Texas Revolution, especially March 2 (Texas Independence Day), March 6 (Battle of the Alamo), and April 21 (Battle of San Jacinto). Since 1905 the DRT has served as the custodial body of the Alamo church, Long Barracks, and adjacent lands (approximately 4.2 acres) (see Daughters of the Republic of Texas: *The Alamo Long Barrack Museum*).

DAVIS, JOHN
Kentucky-born member of Gonzales Ranging Company, 25, who was killed at the Alamo (see Daughters of the Republic of Texas: *The Alamo Long Barrack Museum*).

DAVY CROCKETT AT THE FALL OF THE ALAMO
Sunset production of 1926 starring Cullen Landis (Crockett), Bob Fleming (Bowie), and Joe Rickson (Travis) (see Frank Thompson: *Alamo Movies*).

DAWN AT THE ALAMO
Henry McCardle's 1883 emotionally grotesque painting of the March 6, 1836, battle (see Susan Prendergast Schoelwer: *Alamo Images: Changing Perceptions of a Texas Experience*).

DAY, FREEMAN H. K.
Alamo defender of unknown age and origin who was killed in March 6 battle (see Mary Ann Noonan Guerra: *Heroes of the Alamo and Goliad*).

DAY, JERRY C.
Missouri-born man of unknown age who is currently identified as an Alamo defender based on research by Amelia

Williams. However, recent evidence suggests that Day's name should be removed from the roster of Alamo's defenders (see Thomas R. Lindley: "A Correct List of Alamo Patriots" in *The Alamo Journal*, #89, December 1993).

DAYMON, SQUIRE
Tennessee-born Alamo artillerist, 28, who was killed in the March 6, 1836, battle (see Bill Groneman: *Alamo Defenders*).

DEARDUFF, WILLIAM
Tennessee-born Alamo defender of unknown age who was killed in the March 6, 1836, battle (see Daughters of the Republic of Texas: *The Alamo Long Barrack Museum*).

"DEFEND THE ALAMO!"
Title of 1994 computer disc (MS-DOS version 1.0) war game produced by Incredible Simulations, Inc. of Oak Park, Illinois. Players get the chance to "fire" and "fall back," send out couriers, counter Santa Anna's artillery, and create a Fannin reinforcement scenario, among other options.

DE LA GARZA, ELEXANDRO
Tejano courier of unknown age who served in Juan Seguin's cavarly company who departed from the Alamo before March 6 (see Bill Groneman: *Alamo Defenders*).

DE LEON, ARNOLDO
Author of a number of important books and articles about Texas cultural history, including "Tejanos and the Texas War for Independence: Historiography's Judgment" in the April 1986 edition of the *New Mexico Historical Review*.

DE LUE, DONALD
New Jersey-born sculptor who created the *Edge of Immortality*, a bronze tribute to David Crockett, Jim Bowie, William B. Travis, and James B. Bonham. The sculpture is owned by the Edwin M. Jones Foundation.

DE ZAVALA, ADINA
Historical preservationist and granddaughter of Lorenzo De Zavala, the first vice president of the Republic of Texas, who helped organize fund-raising effort to purchase the Alamo

from commercial interests in 1903. De Zavala, president of the De Zavala chapter of the Daughters of the Republic of Texas (DRT), led a fund-raising effort which raised about $7,000 of the $75,000 selling price. She was assisted by Clara Driscoll of the DRT, who helped raise most of the remaining funds with her own money. Driscoll was later reimbursed the approximate $65,000 sum by the state of Texas. In 1905 the purchased property was given to the state of Texas which, in turn, appointed the DRT as the custodial body for the Alamo. A conflict between De Zavala and Driscoll developed when the latter suggested renting the Long Barracks to some businessmen. De Zavala protested the proposal in February 1908 by remaining in the Long Barracks for three days. The DRT dismissed the De Zavala Chapter from its ranks in 1910. Later, De Zavala founded the Texas Historical Landmarks Association in 1912. Although her efforts saved the Long Barracks, the building's second floor was demolished by order of Lt. Gov. Will Mayes in 1913. Her organization placed thirty-eight historical markers throughout Texas. She died in 1955 and was memorialized in 1994 by a special DRT ceremony at her grave in St. Mary's Cemetery (see Frank Jennings and Rosemary Williams: "Adina De Zavala" in *Texas Highways*, March 1995).

DE ZAVALA, LORENZO
First vice president of the Republic of Texas who served in the 1836 administration of President David G. Burnet (see T.R. Fehrenbach: *Lone Star: A History of Texas and the Texans*).

DENNISON, STEPHEN
Englishman, 24, who was killed at the Alamo on March 6, 1836 (see Walter Lord: *A Time To Stand*).

DeSAUQUE, FRANCIS L.
Pennsylvania-born courier officer (captain) who left the Alamo before the arrival of Santa Anna's troops and departed for Goliad. Although DeSauque left Goliad, he returned there only to be captured with the rest of Fannin's command. DeSaque was executed at Goliad on March 27, 1836 (see Bill Groneman: *Alamo Defenders*).

DeSENSI, ANTHONY M.
Pennsylvania-based artist who created the 1996 painting *Last Stand at the Alamo.*

DESPALLIER, CHARLES
Louisiana-born Alamo courier, 24, who left the mission-fortress after February 25, 1836. He returned with the Gonzales Ranging Company on March 1 and was killed in the assault five days later (see Bill Groneman: *Alamo Defenders*).

DICKINSON, ALMERON
Tennessee-born Alamo artillery officer (captain) who commanded "Come and Take It" gun at Gonzales and later participated in Battle of Béxar. Dickinson sought refuge in the Alamo with his wife, Susanna, and daughter, Angelina, when Santa Anna's troops arrived in San Antonio de Béxar on February 23, 1836. Dickinson was killed in the March 6 battle (see Albert Nofi: *The Alamo and the Texas War for Independence*).

DICKINSON, ANGELINA ELIZABETH
Gonzales, Texas-born (December 14, 1834) daughter of Almeron and Susanna Dickinson who survived the Battle of Alamo with her mother. She married John Maynard Griffith in 1851 and gave birth to three children. Following a divorce she married Oscar Holmes and gave birth to a daughter (see Crystal Sasse Ragsdale: *Women and Children of the Alamo*).

DICKINSON, SUSANNA
Tennessee-born wife of Alamo defender Almeron Dickinson and mother of Angelina Elizabeth Dickinson. Susanna, 22, was the only Anglo woman to survive the March 6 battle. Her account of the Alamo's fall on March 13 verified the report filled by Andres Barcenas and Anselmo Bergaras two days earlier. In later life she remarried four times. Susanna visited the Alamo in 1881 and gave an account of her recollections of the thirteen-day siege and battle (see Bill Groneman: *Eyewitness to the Alamo*).

DILLARD, JOHN HENRY
Tennessee-born Alamo defender, 31, who was killed at the Alamo (see Daughters of the Republic of Texas: *The Alamo Long Barrack Museum*).

DIMITT, PHILIP

Kentucky-born Texian officer who had participated in the capture of Goliad and the Battle of Bexar in 1835 as a company commander. Sent to the Alamo by Houston, Captain Dimitt was utilized by Travis to assess Mexican forces around San Antonio de Béxar on February 23, 1836. He left the area to help bring reinforcements to the Alamo, but following its fall joined Houston's army (see Stephen L. Hardin: *Texian Iliad*).

DIMKINS, JAMES R.

Englishman of unknown age in New Orleans Greys who was killed at the Alamo (see Bill Groneman: *Alamo Defenders*).

"DIRTY HARRY: DUEL FOR CANNONS"

Dane Hartman's 1981 paperback tale of fictitious detective "Dirty Harry" Callahan's shootout with "Sweetboy" in the Alamo 145 years after the 1836 battle.

DOBIE, J. FRANK

Prolific writer of Texas history, including such Alamo-related efforts as "Rose and His Story of the Alamo" in the 1939 edited volume, *The Shadow of History.*

DRAMA OF THE ALAMO, THE

Ramsey Yelvington's 1960 play which was directed by Paul Baker and performed at the San Jose Mission Amphitheatre. The fifty-member cast was composed of members of the Baylor Theater in Waco, Texas.

DRISCOLL, SARAH

So-called "Savior of the Alamo" for her efforts in helping purchase the Alamo property in 1905 before it was sold for commercial purposes. Driscoll donated $65,000 to a fund that was started by Adina de Zavala of the De Zavala Chapter of the Daughters of the Republic of Texas. The fund had raised only some $7,000 until Driscoll made her contribution. In 1905 Driscoll transferred the Alamo land title to the state of Texas, which, in turn, reimbursed her. Her Alamo-saving recollections are found in the 1906 book *In the Shadow of the Alamo.*

DUNCAN, PETER J.
Texian infantry company commander in Col. Francis W. Johnson's Second Division during the Siege and Battle of Béxar in 1835 (see Alwyn Barr: *Texans in Revolt*).

DUQUE, FRANCISCO
Mexican commander of Santa Anna's second assault column against the Alamo on March 6, 1836. Duque's column included some four hundred soldiers of the 1st Toluca and San Luis Potosi battalions. Duque was killed during the predawn battle (see Albert Nofi: *The Alamo and the Texas War for Independence*).

DUVALT, ANDREW
Irishman, 32, from Gonzales who was killed at the Alamo (see Daughters of the Republic of Texas: *The Alamo Long Barrack Museum*).

EASLEY, WILLIAM
Texas-based sculptor who created the bronze, life-sized action sculpture of Alamo defender Toribio Losoya in 1986. The sculpture, which is located on the Paseo Del Alamo near Losoya Street in San Antonio, Texas, depicts Losoya brandishing a pistol in one hand and the flag of 1824 in the other.

EATON, JACK
Field director of the Center for Archaeological Research, The University of Texas at San Antonio, who conducted a March 1977 dig in front of the Alamo church and printed the findings in *Excavations at the Alamo Shrine (Mission San Antonio de Valero)* in 1980.

EDGE OF IMMORTALITY
Bronze sculpture created by New Jersey-born sculptor Donald De Lue featuring David Crockett, Jim Bowie, William B. Travis, and James B. Bonham, which was showcased at the Witte Museum in San Antonio, Texas, for the 1986 exhibit "Remembering the Alamo: The Development of a Texas Symbol, 1836-1936." De Lue is best known for his fourteen-foot bronze of "George Washington at Prayer," which is located in Valley Forge, Pennsylvania.

EDMONDSON, JACK
Texas actor and writer who penned "Victory or Death," the socio-drama performed every March 6 on Alamo Plaza. Edmondson, who portrayed Jim Bowie on TV's *Unsolved Mysteries* in 1995 and the Discovery Channel's *The Battle of The Alamo* in 1996, also compiled and researched (with Dr. Richard Selcer) the *Texas Sesquicentennial Historical Calendar* in 1986.

EDWARDS, H. H.
Texian infantry company commander in Col. Francis W. Johnson's Second Division during Siege and Battle of Béxar in 1835 (see Alwyn Barr: *Texans in Revolt*).

"EL DEGUELLO"
Trumpet selection on American Heritage Record's 1965 *Historic Music of The Great West.* "El Deguello" is the name of the Mexican bugle call that preceeded the predawn March 6, 1836, attack on the Alamo.

EIGENAUER, CONRAD
German-born Alamo defender not currently acknowledged as one who participated in the thirteen-day siege and battle (see Thomas R. Lindley: "A Correct List of Alamo Patriots" in *The Alamo Journal*, #89, December 1993).

1836 REPLICAS
Texas-based diorama firm founded by craftsman James Woolums in 1993. The enterprise specializes in handcrafted replicas of the Alamo.

ENGLISH, GEORGE
Texian infantry captain in Ben Milam's division during the Siege and Battle of Béxar in 1835 (see Alwyn Barr: *Texans in Revolt*).

ESPALIER, CARLOS
Tejano teenager, 17, and Alamo defender who was killed in the March 6, 1836, battle (see Daughters of the Republic of Texas: *The Alamo Long Barrack Museum*).

ESPARZA, ANA SALAZAR DE
Alamo non-combatant and wife of defender Gregorio Es-

parza, who was killed in the March 6, 1836, battle. Esparza and her four children (Enrique, Manuel, Francisco, and Maria) survived the battle and were released by Santa Anna (see Crystal Sasse Ragsdale: *Women and Children of the Alamo*).

ESPARZA, ENRIQUE
Eight-year-old son of Gregorio and Ana Esparza, who survived the Battle of the Alamo. In a 1907 newspaper interview, Esparza said of his recollections of the 1836 siege and battle: "You ask me if I remember it. I tell you yes. It is burned into my brain and indelibly seared there. Neither age nor infirmity could make me forget" (see Crystal Sasse Ragsdale: *Women and Children of the Alamo*).

EVANS, AUGUATA J.
Author of *Inez: A Tale of the Alamo*, an 1871 fictional work about the tragic life of heiress Inez de Garcia.

EVANS, ROBERT
Irishman, 36, and ordnance officer who had served in Col. James C. Neill's command prior to the thirteen-day Alamo siege. Susanna Dickinson said that Major Evans attempted to blow up the Alamo's powder magazine during the March 6 battle (see Mary Ann Noonan Guerra: *Heroes of the Alamo and Goliad*).

EVERETT, EDWARD
Painter of watercolor views of the San Antonio missions in the mid-nineteenth century (see Craig Covner: "Before 1850: A New Look at the Alamo Through Art and Imagery" in *The Alamo Journal*, #70, March 1990).

EWING, JAMES
Georgia-born Alamo artillerist, 24, who was killed at the Alamo (see Thomas R. Lindley: *To Fight the Mexican Eagle: The Ewings of the Texas Revolution*).

"EXCAVATIONS AT THE ALAMO SHRINE"
Special Report booklet #10 printed in 1980 by Jack D. Eaton about a March 1977 dig conducted in front of the Alamo by the Center for Archaeological Research, The University of Texas at San Antonio. Among the uncovered items documented were

flintlock gun flint fragments, lead balls, glass and pottery fragments, and brass and bone buttons.

EYEWITNESS TO THE ALAMO
Bill Groneman's 1996 collection of firsthand accounts describing the Siege and Battle of the Alamo.

EYES OF TEXAS, THE
Don Griffiths-created 1990 color painting of the Alamo church with ghost-like characters of Bonham, Bowie, Travis, Crockett, and Dickinson, along with attacking Mexican soldiers. *The Eyes of Texas* graced the second cover of Bill Groneman's *Alamo Defenders*.

"FALL OF THE ALAMO"
Capt. Rueben M. Potter's 1860 recollection of the Texas Revolution "Printed On The Herald Steam Press" in San Antonio. The idea that Bowie's condition was worsened by a fall at the Alamo was introduced by Potter in this sixteen-page reminiscence, although he denied its accuracy years later (see Walter Lord: *A Time To Stand*).

FALL OF THE ALAMO
Gaston Melies-produced film starring Francis Ford (Crockett) and William Clifford (Travis). This 1911 one-reeler is also known as *The Immortal Alamo* (see Frank Thompson: *Alamo Movies*).

FALL OF THE ALAMO
Military artist Mort Kunstler's 1985 painting that appeared in *The American Spirit*, a book that features over two hundred reproduced paintings. Kunstler portrays Crockett brandishing a sword as he battles near the Alamo church. The artist mistakenly placed a flintlock frizzen on a percussion muzzleloader in the opaque watercolor painting.

FALL OF THE ALAMO, THE
Donald Barr Chidsey-authored 1961 young readers' booklet that was accompanied by colorful art stamps that could be affixed to a number of the pages. Of Crockett's death, the author wrote: "Some of the Texans died right there, among them Davy Crockett, who, with no time to reload, had been laying

about him with a smoking, clubbed Betsy when at last the rush engulfed him."

"FALL OF THE ALAMO: AN ORATION, THE"

Seth Shepard's 1889 pamphlet about the famous siege and battle. Of Crockett's death: "It was near this (artillery) platform after the battle, the body of Davy Crockett was pointed out to Santa Anna, surrounded by heaps of slain Mexicans, some of whom bore marks of his clubbed rifle."

FANNIN, JAMES WALKER

Texian officer, 32, who participated in several 1835 military engagements, including the Gonzales skirmish and the Battle of Béxar. Promoted to colonel, Fannin commanded over four hundred men at Goliad. Travis expected help from Fannin, but his lack of organization and leadership skills resulted in his force's surrender at Coleto Creek and subsequent execution on March 27, 1836 (see Bruce Dettman: "Prisoners Shown No Mercy" in *Wild West,* December 1990).

FEELY, THOMAS F.

New Jersey-based diorama artist who created "Crockett's Last Stand," the most detailed Alamo diorama ever made. The diorama, which features hundreds of 54mm figures, a synchronized audio track, and "exploding" cannons, debuted at the Texas Adventure™ in San Antonio, Texas, on March 4, 1995. Nearly a decade earlier, Feely created the fanciful Alamo diorama, which is currently on display at the Alamo Museum and Gift Shop.

FEHRENBACH, T.R.

Author of a number of books, including the 1968 volume, *Lone Star: A History of Texas and Texans*, which was reprinted as a paperback in 1980.

FILISOLA, VICENTE

Italian major general, 47, in Mexican Army of Operations and second-in-command to Santa Anna. Filisola and his troops arrived at the the Alamo three days after its fall. Following San Jacinto, Filisola was accused of being a traitor for taking his troops back to Mexico (actually Santa Anna's orders) without fighting back against the Texians. Filisola's military memoirs were published in 1848 and translated by Dr. Wallace Woolsey in 1985 (see General Vicente Filisola: *The History of the War in Texas*).

FISHBAUGH, WILLIAM
Alamo defender of unknown age who served in the Gonzales Ranging Company and was killed at the Alamo (see Daughters of the Republic of Texas: *The Alamo Long Barrack Museum*).

FISHER, LEONARD EVERETT
Author of the 1987 book *The Alamo.*

FISHER, REBECCA JANE
Holder of the office of president general of the Daughters of the Republic of Texas longer than any woman since the office was created in 1891. Fisher served from 1908 until 1927. After her tenure, the length of the office was changed to a fixed four-year term until 1935, when it was changed to its present two-year term length.

FLANDERS, JOHN
New Hampshire-born Alamo defender, 36, and member of Gonzales Ranging Company who was killed at the Alamo (see Edward Dubravsky: "John Flanders: Alamo Defender From New Hampshire" in *The Alamo Journal*, #95, February 1995).

FLOYD, DOLPHIN WARD
North Carolina-born Alamo defender, 32, and member of Gonzales Ranging Company who was killed at the Alamo (see Daughters of the Republic of Texas: *The Alamo Long Barrack Museum*).

FORGET THE ALAMO
Wallace O. Chariton's hypothetical volume which rests on the fallacy of fictional questions to suggest the possibilities of Travis' command at Mission Concepcion instead of the Alamo. The author raises such questions as "what if the Alamo had not fallen?"

FONTLEROY, WILLIAM H.
Kentucky-born Alamo defender, 22, who was killed in the March 6, 1836, battle (see Daughters of the Republic of Texas: *The Alamo Long Barrack Museum*).

FORD, JOHN SALMON "RIP"
Member of the Alamo Association and author of 1896 publication, *Origin and Fall of the Alamo, March 6, 1836.*

FOREMAN, GARY
Author of *Crockett: The Gentleman from the Cane* (1986) and founder of the San Antonio Living History Association who created a controversial twenty-page renovation plan in 1984 via his Alamo Plaza Historic Task Force organization. The task force's goal was to help improve the educational and historical interpretation of the Alamo. Foreman's plan, although initially criticized by such groups as the Daughters of the Republic of Texas, later became the central objective of his Alamo Foundation. Some of Foreman's suggestions were later studied by the Alamo Plaza Study Committee in 1994 (see Lianne Hart: "The Daughters of Texas Have A Curt Rebuke For A Yankee Who Remembers The Alamo — Forget It" in *People,* June 4, 1984).

FORSYTH, JOHN HUBBARD
New York-born Alamo cavalry officer, 38, who accompanied Lt. Col. William Barrett Travis to the the Alamo in January 1836. Captain Forsyth was killed in the March 6, 1836, battle (see Bill Groneman: *Alamo Defenders*).

"FRANKIE AVALON AS 'SMITTY' SINGS SONGS OF *THE ALAMO*"
Chancellor Records extended-play recording featuring 1950s pop music idol Frankie Avalon, who appeared in John Wayne's *The Alamo* as "Smitty." Following the release of the film in 1960, the four-song recording was issued. It included "Ballad of the Alamo," "Tennessee Babe (Oh, Lisa)," "Green Leaves of Summer," and "Here's to the Ladies" (see "Alamo EP Discovered" in *The Alamo News,* #45, July 1985).

FRANKS, NIDLAND
Captain of artillery in Ben Milam's First Division during the Siege and Battle of Béxar in 1835 (see Alwyn Barr: *Texans in Revolt*).

FUENTES, ANTONIO
Tejano member of Juan Seguin's cavalry company, 22, who was killed at the Alamo (see Daughters of the Republic of Texas: *The Alamo Long Barrack Museum*).

FUQUA, GALBA
Alabama-born Alamo defender, 16, who was killed in the March 6, 1836, battle (see Daughters of the Republic of Texas: *The Alamo Long Barrack Museum*).

FUNERAL PYRE, THE
Jose Arpa's painting of the burning of the Alamo defenders which graced the cover of Virgil Baugh's 1985 Bison Book, *Rendezvous at the Alamo.* Santa Anna ordered the bodies of the Alamo dead burned following the March 6, 1836, battle.

FURIES, THE
Volume IV of John Jakes' 1976 American Bicentennial series which features an early section on the Siege and Battle of the Alamo. Of Crockett's death, one character, Sam, noted: "Colonel Crockett went down with ten, maybe twenty on top of him."

FUSILEROS COMPANY
Mexican line infantry company in Santa Anna's army during the Texas Revolution. The *fusileros* companies usually numbered six within an eight-company regiment.

GAONA, COL. ANTONIO
Commander of Santa Anna's First Brigade, which included the Aldama Permanente Infantry Battalion and the Zapadores Battalion, among other units (Albert Nofi: *The Alamo and the Texas War for Independence*).

GARNETT, WILLIAM
Virginia-born Alamo defender, 23, who was killed during the March 6, 1836, battle (see Bill Groneman: *Alamo Defenders*).

GARRAND, JAMES W.
Twenty-three-year-old Louisianan who participated in 1835 Battle of Béxar and died at the Battle of the Alamo (see Bill Groneman: *Alamo Defenders*).

GARRETT, JAMES G.
Tennessee-born, 30-year-old member of New Orleans Grays who died at the Battle of the Alamo (see Bill Groneman: *Alamo Defenders*).

GARVIN, JOHN E.
Gonzales artillerist, 27, who served under Capt. William Carey and died at the Battle of the Alamo (see Bill Groneman: *Alamo Defenders*).

GASTON, JOHN
Teenager, 17, who served in Gonzales Ranging Company and who died at the Battle of the Alamo (see Bill Groneman: *Alamo Defenders*).

GENTILZ, JEAN LOUIS THEODORE
French-born painter who came to San Antonio in 1843 and painted *Fall of the Alamo* ca.1885. The original work was destroyed in a fire in 1906, the same year that the painter died (see Susan Prendergast Schoelwer: *Alamo Images: Changing Perceptions of a Texas Experience*).

GEORGE, DAVID
Houston-based business developer who (along with Jose J. Carrasquillo and Stanley F. Buchthal) in 1993 launched The Texas Adventure,™ a multi-media Encountarium ®, in San Antonio (across the street from the Alamo). The Texas Adventure™ features a special effects battle with animatronic and 3-D ghost-like images of Alamo defenders (see review by Dan R. Goddard in *San Antonio Express-News*, 1-J, June 26, 1994).

GEORGE, JAMES
Thirty-four-year-old member of the Gonzales Ranging Company who died at the Battle of the Alamo. His wife, Elizabeth, was the sister of another Alamo defender, William Dearduff (see Bill Groneman: *Alamo Defenders*).

GEORGE, WILLIAM
Alamo defender not currently recognized as such. According to Thomas R. Lindley of Texian Army Investigations, George is one of a number of men who should be added to the Alamo's roll call.

GEORGIA BATTALION

U.S.-raised military unit commanded by Lt. Col. William Ward, who led the force against Mexican troops at Refugio on March 13, 1836 (see Bill and Marjorie K. Walraven: *The Magnificent Barbarians: Little Told Tales of the Texas Revolution*).

GILES, ALFRED

Famous architect who was supposed to design a 165-foot tall monument for the Alamo Monument Association in the early twentieth century. The plan never materialized. In 1912 Giles offered his own plan: an 802-foot high column that would rise from a museum base featuring displays from 254 Texas counties. Huge 30-foot statues of Davy Crockett, Jim Bowie, William B. Travis, and James B. Bonham would embellish the column's base. The towering structure was never built.

GILKYSON, TERRY

Musician whose band Terry Gilkyson and the Easy Riders released *Remember The Alamo* in 1960 to coincide with the release of John Wayne's film *The Alamo* (see Donald Clark and Christopher Andersen: *John Wayne's The Alamo*).

GILLIS, DON

Creator of 1947 symphonic poem, "The Alamo," part of a trilogy on symbols of American freedom. According to Gillis, his composition was "an attempt to portray musically the deep feelings of emotion that arise in the contemplation of the heroism and courage expressed by the defenders of the Alamo as they gave their lives in the defense of freedom." Gillis conducted the New Symphony Orchestra for a 1950 London Records recording release.

"GLEASON'S PICTORAL DRAWING ROOM COMPANION"

In 1854 this publication printed *Ruins of the Church of El Alamo*, which was based on a view of the mission-fortress by U.S. Army artist Edward Everett. The image in "Gleason's" features a horse-drawn carriage and several tourists who are drawn too small to scale (see Susan Prendergast Schoelwer: *Alamo Images, Changing Perceptions of a Texas Experience*).

GLORIOUS DEFIANCE: LAST STANDS THROUGH-OUT HISTORY

Dennis Karl's 1990 book, which includes a section of the Siege and Battle of the Alamo. Of Crockett's death, the author re-states the Nunez account about a defender who could have been the famous ex-congressman: "He sprang at him and dealt him a deadly blow with his sword, just above the right eye, which felled him to the ground, and in an instant he was pierced by no less than twenty bayonets."

"GOING TO THE ALAMO"

Proposed but never filmed, Rex Sparger-produced, 20-hour, 1986 TV mini series (see Frank Thompson: *Alamo Movies*).

GOLIAD, CAPTURE OF

On October 10, 1835, Capt. George M. Collinsworth's forty-seven men defeated the twenty-eight-man Mexican garrison at Goliad (*Presidio La Bahia*) and captured its military stores (see James W. Pohl and Stephen L. Hardin: "The Military History of the Texas Revolution: An Overview" in *Southwestern Historical Quarterly*, 89, January 1986).

GOLIAD MASSACRE

On March 27, 1836, Col. James W. Fannin's command was executed by a Mexican force commanded by Gen. Jose Urrea after surrendering a week earlier following the Battle of Coleto Creek. Despite the escape of several dozen men, the event was called the "Goliad Massacre" and cries of "Remember Goliad" as well as "Remember the Alamo" were shouted by Houston's victorious troops at San Jacinto on April 21, 1836 (see Kathryn Stoner O'Conner: *Presido La Bahia*).

"GONE TO TEXAS"

Video title of 1986 TV movie *Houston: The Legend of Texas*, which starred Sam Elliott in the title role. The Peter Levin-directed film, which focused on Houston's adult life up through the Texas Revolution, included an Alamo aftermath scene (shot at Happy Shahan's Alamo Village in Brackettville, Texas, site of the John Wayne film, *The Alamo*), in which the bodies of the principal dead Alamo defenders (Travis, Crockett, and Bowie) are identified and five others executed (see Frank Thompson: *Alamo Movies*).

GONE TO TEXAS

Final title in Jason Manning's fictional frontier trilogy. The 1995 paperback contains this error-filled commentary: "In 1839, when President Andrew Jackson decides it is time for Texas to gain its independence from Mexico, he calls upon Flintlock Jones and his grandson Christopher Groves." The book concludes with the 1832 insurrection at Anahuac.

GONZALES, PETRA

Elderly female noncombatant, known also as Nena, who survived the Siege and Battle of the Alamo (see Crystal Sasse Ragsdale: *Women and Children of the Alamo*).

GONZALES, BATTLE OF

Skirmish of October 2, 1835, when a Mexican cavalry company was thwarted in its efforts to retrieve a cannon which had been given to the citizens of Gonzales several years earlier as a weapon to counter Comanche attacks. The small Texian force taunted the approaching Mexican force with a flag bearing a picture of the artillery piece and the words "Come And Take It." This conflict, sometimes called the "Lexington" of the Texas Revolution, marked the beginning of fighting between Mexican and Texian forces (see Stephen L. Hardin: *Texian Iliad*).

GONZALES "COME AND TAKE IT" CANNON

The six-pound artillery piece portrayed in art as a relatively small caliber piece mounted on large cart-like wooden wheels that was the target of advancing Mexican cavalry troops on October 2, 1835, at Gonzales. The gun was buried eleven days later near Sandies Creek. The gun was allegedly unearthed in the summer of 1936 following a flood and later verified in 1979-1980 by Dr. Pat Wagner of Shiner, Texas. Thomas Ricks Lindley of Texian Army Investigations suggests, however, that the "Come And Take It" gun has yet to be found (see Jane Bradfield: *RX Take One Cannon*).

GONZALES 32
Military unit, formally called the Gonzales Ranging Company, which came to the defense of the Alamo on March 1, 1836. Unit was commanded by George Kimball. Thomas R. Lindley of Texian Army Investigations suggests that the total of thirty-two men was probably higher (see Stephen L. Hardin: *Texian Iliad*).

GOODRICH, JOHN C.
Virginia-born twenty-seven-year-old defender who fought at the Alamo. Four days before his death, Goodrich's brother, Benjamin Briggs Goodrich, signed the Texas Declaration of Independence (see Bill Groneman: *Alamo Defenders*).

GRAHAM, C. B.
Lithographer who reproduced Edward Everett's drawing of the Alamo in the nineteenth century as *Ruins of the Church of the Alamo* (see Susan Prendergast Schoelwer: *Alamo Images, Changing Perceptions of a Texas Experience*).

GRANADEROS COMPANY
Mexican grenadier infantry company of Santa Anna's army during the Texas Revolution. The *granaderos* company was one of eight companies within an infantry regiment.

GRENET, HONORE
French-born businessman who purchased the two-story long barracks and adjacent property from the Catholic Church on November 30, 1877, for his large retail store, which carried everything from boots and beer to groceries and tobacco. Grenet, who also leased the Alamo church as a warehouse, died in 1882. His Alamo properties were subsequently sold at public auction for $28,000 on January 23, 1886, to Charles Hugo, Gustav Schmeltzer, and William Heurmann (see Frederick Charles Chabot: *The Alamo: Mission, Fortress and Shrine*).

GRIFFITHS, DON
California-based artist who painted *The Eyes of Texas*, which features the ghost-like images of Bonham, Bowie, Travis, Crockett, and Dickinson, and the Mexican army against the modern-day Alamo church. Griffiths, who won the 1986 "Artist of the Year" award from the California Wildlife Con-

federation, also created *Defense of a Legend,* which depicts Crockett's final moments before the doors of the Alamo church. The painting also graces the cover of author Bill Groneman's book of the same name.

GROCE, JARED
Wealthy agriculturalist whose plantation, situated some twenty miles north of San Felipe, was used by Gen. Sam Houston's army as a training camp of sorts for two weeks in early April (see David Nevin: *The Texans*).

GROCE'S LANDING
A steamboat landing dock on the Brazos River property of Jared Groce. On April 12, Houston utilized the steamboat *Yellowstone* to transfer his troops to the eastern shore of the Brazos River (see Stephen L. Hardin: *Texian Iliad*).

GRONEMAN, BILL
New York-based writer who co-authored (with Phil Rosenthal) *Roll Call at the Alamo,* and authored *Alamo Defenders; Defense of a Legend; Eyewitness to the Alamo;* and numerous periodical articles. In *Defense of a Legend,* the author suggests that David Crockett died fighting at the Alamo.

G.T.T.
Contemporary abbreviation for "Gone To Texas," a phrase frequently carved into wooden doors or walls which indicated that the resident had moved "lock, stock and barrel" to Texas (see Bill and Marjorie K. Walraven: *The Magnificent Barbarians: Little Told Tales of the Texas Revolution*).

GUERRERO, BRIGIDO
Tejano who allegedly survived the Battle of the Alamo by convincing Mexican soldiers that he was a Texian prisoner (see Walter Lord: *A Time to Stand*).

GWYNNE, JAMES C.
English born thirty-two-year-old artillerist in Captain Carey's company and veteran of the Siege and Battle of Bexar who died at the Alamo (see Bill Groneman: *Alamo Defenders*).

HANDY, R. E.
Texian scout ordered by Sam Houston to accompany Erastus

"Deaf" Smith and Henry Carnes in order to verify Anselmo Bergaras and Andres Barcenas' report that the Alamo had fallen (see Albert Nofi: *The Alamo and the Texas War for Independence*).

HANNUM, JAMES

Pennsylvania-born defender, 20, who died at the Alamo (see Bill Groneman: *Alamo Defenders*).

HARDIN, STEPHEN L.

Victoria College (Victoria, Texas) historian who authored the award-winning *Texian Iliad* (1994) and numerous articles for such publications as the *New Handbook of Texas; The Alamo Journal;* and *Military History: Past and Present,* among others.

HARRELL, WILLIAM

Alamo defender not currently acknowledged as one who participated in the thirteen-day siege and battle. An 1846 document lists thirty-three men as "Killed at the Alamo" or "With Travis." All the names can be found on other extant Alamo rosters except for seven. Of these men, five were at Goliad and two, William Harrell and James R. Munson, probably died at the Alamo (see Thomas R. Lindley: "A Correct List of Alamo Patriots" in *The Alamo Journal,* #89, December 1993).

HARRIS, JOHN

Kentucky-born defender, 23, member of the Gonzales Ranging Company who died at the Alamo (see Bill Groneman: *Alamo Defenders*).

HARRISON, ANDREW JACKSON

Tennessee-born defender, 27, who died at the Alamo (see Bill Groneman: *Alamo Defenders*).

HARRISON, I. L. K.

Alamo defender not currently acknowledged as participating in the thirteen-day siege and battle (see Thomas R. Lindley: "A Correct List of Alamo Patriots" in *The Alamo Journal,* #89, December 1993).

HARRISON, WILLIAM B.

Ohio-born commander, 25, of Tennessee Mounted Volunteers who died at the Alamo (see Bill Groneman: *Alamo Defenders*).

HARTMAN, DANE
Author of 1981 paperback, *Dirty Harry: Duel For Cannons*, a fictional tale about the .44 Magnum-carrying detective who shoots it out with "Sweetboy" in the Alamo.

HARVEY, LAURENCE
Lithuanian-born actor who played William Barret Travis in *The Alamo* (1960). In the film, Harvey's Travis did not draw "the line" (see Donald Clark and Christopher Andersen: *John Wayne's The Alamo*).

HAUCK, RICHARD BOYD
University of West Florida (Pensacola) historian who authored *Crockett, A Bio-Bibliography* in 1982. The book features an Alamo-related section titled "The Many Deaths of Crockett."

HAUNTED ALAMO: A HISTORY OF THE MISSION AND A GUIDE TO PARANORMAL ACTIVITY
Rob and Anne Wlodarski's 1996 book (G-Host Publishing) about the spirits who have haunted the Alamo since the first "documented" vision in 1894.

HAWKINS, CHARLES E.
Texian captain of the *Independence*, a Texian ten-gun schooner. Following a successful mission to Tampico, Mexico, Hawkins was promoted to commodore and led a small squadron of privateers around the Matagorda Bay area in March and April 1836 (see Albert Nofi: *The Alamo and the Texas War for Independence*).

HAWKINS, JOSEPH M.
Irishman, 37, who died at the Battle of the Alamo (see Bill Groneman: *Alamo Defenders*).

HAYDEN, STERLING
New Jersey-born character actor who played Jim Bowie in *The Last Command* (1955) (see Frank Thompson: *Alamo Movies*).

HAYS, JOHN M.
Tennessee-born defender, 22, who died at the Alamo (see Bill Groneman: *Alamo Defenders*).

HAYTHORNTHWAITE, PHILIP
British military historian who authored the 1986 booklet, *The Alamo and the War of Texan Independence, 1835-36.*

HEDGCOCK, RICHARD
Painter who created *The Decision* (1994), a painting depicting Travis drawing the line in front of the Alamo's palisade area. The painting was reproduced as a water bottle label for North Carolina's Le Bleu Corporation in the mid-1990s.

HEISKELL, CHARLES M.
Tennessee-born defender, 23, who died at the Alamo (see Bill Groneman: *Alamo Defenders*).

HERNDON, PATRICK HENRY
Virginia-born defender, 34, who died at the Alamo (see Bill Groneman: *Alamo Defenders*).

HEROES OF THE ALAMO
Edited 1956 collection of documents, poems, songs, photographs, etc. by A. Garland Adair and M. H. Crockett, a third cousin of the famous Alamo defender. Much of the book's information came from the article "Travis, Bowie, Bonham and Davy Crockett" in the January 1956 issue of *Under Texas Skies*.

HEROES OF THE ALAMO
Sunset Production film of 1937 which focused on the Alamo's only Anglo couple, "Al" Dickinson (Bruce Warren) and "Anne" Dickinson (Ruth Findlay) (see Frank Thompson: *Alamo Movies*).

HERRERA, BLAS
Cousin of Juan Seguin who first spotted Santa Anna's army cross the Rio Grande into Texas in February 1836 (see Walter Lord: *A Time To Stand*).

Alamo defenders battle Mexican soldiers in Heroes of the Alamo (1937).
From the collection of Dr. Murray Weissmann.

HIGHSMITH, BENJAMIN FRANKLIN
Missouri Territory-born courier, 18, who departed from the Alamo prior to March 6 and participated in the Battle of San Jacinto (see Walter Lord: *A Time To Stand*).

HIRSCHFELD, BURT
Author of 1966 book *After the Alamo: The Story of the   Mexican War.*

HISTORY, BATTLES AND FALL OF THE ALAMO
L. F. Meyers' 1896 publication about the Alamo that included a "points of interest" section on San Antonio, Texas.

HISTORICAL SKETCH AND GUIDE TO THE ALAMO
Leonora Bennett's 1904 publication, which includes commentary on the Siege and Battle of the Alamo. Of Crockett's death: "Crockett was among the last to die. His 'Betsy' made many a Mexican rue the day he had found the army, and when there was no more time to load he clubbed many a foe to death with his gun before he finally succumbed, his body bullet-ridden for minutes before he gave up the struggle."

HOLLAND, TAPLEY
Ohio-born artillerist in Captain Carey's company, 26, who died at the Alamo (see Bill Groneman: *Alamo Defenders*).

HOLLOWAY, JAMES
Alamo defender not currently acknowledged as one who participated in the thirteen-day siege and battle (see Thomas R. Lindley: "A Correct List of Alamo Patriots" in *The Alamo Journal*, #89, December 1993).

HOLLOWAY, SAMUEL
Pennsylvania-born member of New Orleans Grays, 28, who died at the Alamo (see Bill Groneman: *Alamo Defenders*).

HOLLYWOOD AND AMERICAN HISTORY
Compiled by Michael R. Pitts, this 1984 volume states: ". . . the major fault of (John Wayne's) *The Alamo* is that it is too long and too full of contrived situations before the climactic battle."

HORTON, ALBERT C.

Colonel in Fannin's command who participated in a series of inconclusive cavalry skirmishes on March 18 near Goliad (see Albert Nofi: *The Alamo and the Texas War for Independence*).

HOUSTON, SAM

Tennessee-born commander of Texas forces, 43, who avenged the Alamo and Goliad at San Jacinto, April 21, 1836. Following David G. Burnet's term as President *ad interim* of Texas, Houston won the highest office of the young republic as a result of votes cast on the September 1, 1836, general election. He was inaugurated on October 22, 1836. He was elected to the presidency again in 1841 and served as one of the state's first U. S. senators after Texas joined the Union. He was elected governor in 1859 but opposed secession. He died in 1863 (see Alfred M. Williams: *Sam Houston and the War for Independence in Texas*).

HOUSTON: THE LEGEND OF TEXAS

1986 TV movie whose title was later changed to *Gone To Texas* for the home videocassette market. The production, starring Sam Elliott in the title role, featured an Alamo aftermath scene in which five defenders are executed. Crockett's dead body is seen prior to the firing squad sequence. The TV movie, which was filmed at Alamo Village in Brackettville, Texas, was given the Wrangler Award by the Western Heritage Museum and Cowboy Hall of Fame in 1987 (see Frank Thompson: *Alamo Movies*).

HOW DID DAVY DIE?

Authored by Dan Kilgore, former president of the Texas State Historical Association, this small book supported Jose Enrique de la Peña's account of Crockett's death, i.e., he was captured with six others and executed on March 6, 1836. *How Did Davy Die?* was generally not well received by those who believed Crockett died fighting (see Susan Prendergast Schoelwer: *Alamo Images: Changing Perceptions of a Texas Experience*).

HOWELL, WILLIAM D.

Massachusetts-born physician, 45, who died at the Alamo dur-

Sam Houston. Illustration by Gary Zaboly.

ing the March 6, 1836, battle (see Bill Groneman: *Alamo Defenders*).

HUBERMAN, BRIAN
Film and video historian specializing in the Alamo. The Rice University-based Huberman created a forty-minute documentary on the making of John Wayne's *The Alamo* that was included in the expanded "director's cut" of the film when it was released in its videocassette format in 1992.

HUGO & SCHMELTZER
Merchandise company which acquired Long Barracks property from Honore Grenet's estate following a public auction for $28,000 on January 23, 1886, when Charles Hugo, Gustav Schmeltzer, and William Heurmann bought it. The Hugo & Schmeltzer Company assumed ownership of the property on May 12, 1900. Hugo took complete control of the site on September 26, 1903. He later later sold it on February 10, 1904, to Clara Driscoll for $75,000, following an attempt by the Daughters of the Republic of Texas to raise the necessary funds (see Frederick C. Chabot: *The Alamo: Mission, Fortress and Shrine*).

HULL, JOHN
Connecticut-based painter who displayed twenty-six Alamo acrylics at New York's Grace Borgenicht Gallery in 1994. Among Hull's paintings were *Fall of the Alamo; Death of Crockett; Shootout at the Long Barracks;* and *Confrontation: Bowie and Travis* (see William Chemerka "Alamo Painting Exhibit" in *The Alamo Journal*, #83, July 1994).

HUNNICUTT, ARTHUR
Character actor who portrayed David Crockett in the 1955 film *The Last Command* (1955) (see Frank Thompson: *Alamo Movies*).

HUTCHINSON, T. P.
Alamo defender not currently acknowledged as one who participated in the thirteen-day siege and battle (see Thomas R. Lindley: "A Correct List of Alamo Patriots" in *The Alamo Journal*, #89, December 1993).

HUTTON, PAUL ANDREW
University of New Mexico historian who authored a number of articles on the Alamo and David Crockett. He penned introductions for *Alamo Images: Changing Perceptions of a Texas Experience* and the reprint of *A Narrative of the Life of David Crockett of the State of Tennessee.* Hutton, who believes Crockett was executed following the Battle of the Alamo, is preparing a major historical biography of the famous frontiersman.

IMMORTAL ALAMO, THE
Gaston Melies-produced silent film (1911) which starred Otto Meyer (Crockett) and William Clifford (Travis). Melies, brother of famous French filmmaker George Melies, appears in the one-reel film as "Padre" (see Frank Thompson: *Texas' First Picture Show*).

IN THE ALAMO
Opie Read's 1900 work of fiction about the Siege and Battle of the Alamo. Of Crockett's death: "'. . . and out there,'" she added, waving her hand, "'is where old Crockett was found, surrounded by his enemies.'"

INDEPENDENCE
A 10-gun schooner in the first Texas navy (see Albert Nofi: *The Alamo and the Texas War for Independence*).

INDEPENDENCE DAY
Texas declared itself independent of Mexico on March 2, 1836, at Washington-on-the-Brazos where fifty-eight delegates stated that ". . . the people of Texas do now constitute a Free, Sovereign and Independent Republic . . ." (see Wallace O. Chariton: *100 Days in Texas, the Alamo Letters*).

INEZ: A TALE OF THE ALAMO
Fictional work penned by Augusta J. Evans in 1871 about heiress Inez de Garcia. Of Crockett's death, Evans wrote that Fannin (spelled Fanning) lamented at Goliad with the following: "Oh, Crockett! Bowie! can I do better than follow thy example and give my life in this true cause?"

INVINCIBLE

Flagship of first Texas navy. The eighty-four-foot schooner, which assisted Sam Houston in capturing weapons from the Mexicans in the Gulf of Mexico following the fall of the Alamo, sank on August 28, 1837, at Galveston, but was found on August 8, 1995, by members of the National Underwater and Marine Agency (see "Wreckage of Texas navy ship that aided Sam Houston believed found" in *The Dallas Morning News*, August 23, 1995).

INHERIT THE ALAMO

Author Holly Brear's anthropological study of the Alamo and the sociological groups that relate to it. The 1995 book's subtitle is *Myth and Ritual at an American Shrine*, which reflects the author's treatment of the various parades, commemorations, and celebrations that take place annually at the Shrine of Texas Liberty.

IN THE SHADOW OF THE ALAMO

Clara Driscoll's 1906 publication which includes a brief history of the Alamo and her recollections of how she assisted in purchasing the famous mission-fortress for Texas.

JACKSON, ANDREW

President of the United States during the Texas Revolution. Although the Jackson administration did not officially encourage the independence movement against Mexico, it was aware of Sam Houston's territorial aspirations with regards to Texas. The United States under Jackson finally recognized the Republic of Texas as an independent state in March of 1837.

JACKSON, MICHAEL

World famous musical performer who was identified in 1987 as being interested in buying the Alamo for $20 million after his alleged plan to buy John ("The Elephant Man") Merrick's bones fell through (see *Detroit News*: "Alamo not for sale," July 30, 1987).

JACKSON, RON

Author of 1997 book *Alamo Legacy: Alamo Descendants Remember the Alamo*.

JACKSON, THOMAS

Irish member of Gonzales Ranging Company (age unknown) who died at the Alamo (see Bill Groneman: *Alamo Defenders*).

JACKSON, WILLIAM DANIEL

Kentucky artillerist, 29, who died at the Alamo (see The Daughters of the Republic of Texas: *The Alamo Long Barrack Museum*).

JAKES, JOHN

Author of the 1976 book, *The Furies* (volume IV of the American Bicentennial series), which featured a Siege and Battle of the Alamo section. Jakes also penned the children's book *Susanna of the Alamo* in 1986.

JAMES A. MICHENER'S "TEXAS"

Two-part 1995 TV movie based upon the Michener novel, *Texas*. Originally released in late 1994 as a videocassette, this critically panned production featured David Keith (Bowie), Grant Show (Travis), John Schneider (Crockett), and Lloyd Battista (Santa Anna). The movie's Alamo scenes were filmed at Alamo Village in Brackettville, Texas, the place where John Wayne's *The Alamo* was filmed.

JAMESON, GREEN B.

Kentucky-born, 29, chief engineer of Alamo garrison who provided a description of the mission fortress to Houston in January 1836. He perished in the March 6 assault (see Stephen L. Hardin: *Texian Iliad*).

JENNINGS, BENTON

Texas actor who portrayed William B. Travis in *Travis*, a 1991 Grace Products Corporation production. *Travis* was filmed at Alamo Village in Brackettville, Texas, the site of John Wayne's 1960 film, *The Alamo*.

JENNINGS, GORDON C.

Pennsylvania-born defender, 56 (oldest in the Alamo garrison), who died during the March 6 assault. His brother, Charles, was executed at Goliad on March 27, 1836 (see Bill Groneman: *Alamo Defenders*).

JIMENEZ BATTALION

Veteran Mexican infantry unit in Brig. Gen. Joaquin Ramierez y Sesma's brigade (see Albert Nofi: *The Alamo and the Texas War for Independence*).

JIMENES, DAMACIO

Tejano Alamo defender of unknown age who participated in the Battle of Béxar and was killed in the March 6, 1836, assault (see William Chemerka: "Damacio Jimenez: A New Name to the Alamo's Roll Call" in *The Alamo Journal*, #56, June 1987).

JOE

Travis' slave who resided in Harrisburg, Texas, prior to the Texas Revolution. Joe took part in the Battle of the Alamo and survived, accompanying Susannah and Angelina Dickinson to Sam Houston's camp (see Walter Lord: *A Time To Stand*).

JOHN

Alamo defender without a documented last name who died during the March 6, 1836, battle. Extant documentation does not support his alleged status as a slave (see Thomas R. Lindley: "A Correct List of Alamo Patriots" in *The Alamo Journal*, #89, December 1993).

JOHNSON, LEWIS

Welschman, 26, who died at the Alamo (see Daughters of the Republic of Texas: *The Alamo Long Barrack Museum*).

JOHNSON, WILLIAM

Pennsylvania-born defender of unknown age who died at the Alamo (see Bill Groneman: *Alamo Defenders*).

JOHNSON, WILLIAM P.

Possible Alamo courier who perished at Goliad (see Bill Groneman: *Alamo Defenders*).

JONES, MRS. ANSON

First president general of the Daughters of the Republic of Texas. She served from 1891 until 1908, the second longest tenure (next to Rebecca Jane Fisher) among all the presidents general.

JONES, JOHN
New York-born Alamo officer who died during March 6, 1836, assault (see Bill Groneman: *Alamo Defenders*).

JULIA, RAUL
Actor who played Santa Anna in *The Alamo: 13 Days To Glory* in 1987 (see Frank Thompson: *Alamo Movies*).

KANE, THOMAS, J.
Editor of the 1960 Sovereign Publication *The Alamo*, a promotional souvenir book which coincided with the release of John Wayne's epic film of the same name. Wayne and Donald L. LaCava served as the book's publishers.

KARL, DENNIS
Author of the 1990 book *Glorious Defiance: Last Stands Throughout History,* which features a section of the Siege and Battle of the Alamo.

KARNES, HENRY
Texian scout ordered by Sam Houston to accompany Erastus "Deaf" Smith and R. E. Handy to verify story of Anselmo Bargaras and Andres Barcenas that the Alamo had fallen (see Albert Nofi: *The Alamo and the Texas War for Independence*).

KEITH, BRIAN
Actor who played Davy Crockett in the 1987 TV movie *The Alamo: 13 Days To Glory* (see Frank Thompson: *Alamo Movies*).

KEITH, DAVID
Actor who played Jim Bowie in the 1995 TV movie *James A. Michener's "Texas."*

KELLOGG, JOHN BENJAMIN
Kentucky teenage resident of Gonzales, 19, who is incorrectly identified at the Alamo as a member of the Gonzales Ranging Company. Kellogg did not die at the Alamo; he died in Harrisburg, Texas, in late 1836 (see Thomas R. Lindley: "A Correct List of Alamo Patriots" in *The Alamo Journal,* #89, December 1993).

KENNY, JAMES
Virginia-born defender, 22, who died at the Alamo (see Bill Groneman: *Alamo Defenders*).

KENT, ANDREW
Kentucky-born member of the Gonzales 32 (estimated age: 34-38) who died at the Alamo (see Bill Groneman: *Alamo Defenders*).

KERL, SIMON
Author of the 1868 *Storming of the Alamo*. The author does not mention the death of David Crockett.

KERR, JOSEPH
Louisiana-born defender, 22, who died at the Alamo (see Bill Groneman: *Alamo Defenders*).

KILGORE, DAN
Former president of the Texas State Historical Association in 1977 and author of *How Did Davy Die?* the following year. Kilgore supported Jose Enrique de la Peña's account of Crockett's death and, as a result, generated much criticism from supporters of the famous frontiersman at the time of his publication (see Susan Prendergast Schoelwer: *Alamo Images: Changing Perceptions of a Texas Experience*).

KIMBALL, GEORGE
Pennsylvania-born commander, 33, of Gonzales 32 who died at the Alamo (see Walter Lord: *A Time To Stand*).

KING, WILLIAM PHILIP
Teenage member of Gonzales 32 who died at the Alamo (see Walter Lord: *A Time To Stand*).

KNAGGS, JOHN R.
Author of 1977 historical novel *The Bugles are Silent*, which presents both the Texian and Mexican sides of the War for Texas Independence.

KUNSTLER, MORT
Well-known modern military artist who created the Alamo battle scene dust jacket art for recent editions of T. R. Fehrenbach's *Lone Star: A History of Texas and the Texans*.

KWIK-KOPY CORPORATION
Cypress, Texas-based international photocopy firm which built a full-scale Alamo-like facade on its fourteen-thousand-square-foot training center in 1985. The corporate structure, named "Alamo II," is seemingly identical to the original, except for incorrect spiraling on its front columns (see Tom Walker's "Success, Failure, Bud Hadfield, and the American Bald Eagle" in *The Continental*, October 1985).

LADIES AT THE ALAMO
Paul Zindel's play about a backstage leadership feud at the new "Alamo Theatre" in Texas City, Texas. The two-act play debuted on April 7, 1977, in New York, but it has actually nothing to do with the historic Alamo. However, Zindel titled Act One "The Ambush" and Act Two "The Massacre." Furthermore, the play notes that the old "Alamo Theatre" existed in an old converted church.

LAMEGO, MIGUEL A. SANCHEZ
Author of *The Siege and Taking of the Alamo* in 1968, which was translated by Consuelo Velasco. Lamego provides various conflicting accounts of Crockett's death and suggests that readers make their "own conclusions."

LANDRUM, WILLIAM
Texian infantry captain in Ben Milam's First Division during Siege and Battle of Béxar in 1835 (see Alwyn Barr: *Texans in Revolt*).

LARSON, GARY
Off-beat cartoonist who drew several Alamo-related creations in his "The Far Side" series prior to his retirement at the end of 1994.

LAST COMMAND, THE
Republic Pictures film (1955) of the Siege and Battle of the Alamo starring Sterling Hayden (Bowie), Richard Carlson (Travis), Arthur Hunnicutt (Crockett), and J. Carroll Naish (Santa Anna) (see Frank Thompson: *Alamo Movies*).

LAST NIGHT AT THE ALAMO
Director Eagle Pennell's 1984 film about a group of beer

drinkers who unsuccessfully try to save their favorite Houston saloon, called the Alamo, from encroaching commercial development. Kathleen Carroll of the *New York Daily News* gave the unrated film two and a half stars.

LAST STAND AT THE ALAMO
Author Aden R. Carter's 1990 children's book which features a number of maps, photographs, and paintings. Of Crockett's death: "One Mexican account says that Crockett died near the south wall. Another says that he found shelter in the long barracks along the east wall."

LAST STAND AT THE ALAMO
Anthony M. DeSensi's 1996 painting of the fight between Mexican soldiers and Crockett's men in the chapel courtyard.

LAST STANDS
Craig Philip's 1994 volume (complete title: *Last Stands: Famous Battles Against the Odds*) that includes a ten-page section on the Alamo.

LA VILLITA
Some two dozen assorted buildings that extended south of the Alamo. *La Villita* was the scene of some fighting on February 25 during the Alamo siege (see David Nevin: *The Texans*).

LEAGUE OF UNITED LATIN AMERICAN CITIZENS (LULAC)
Organization which criticized the way Hispanics were portrayed during the 1987 filming of *Alamo . . . The Price of Freedom*. Some members of LULAC later staged a picket line protest outside the IMAX Rivercenter theater when the giant-screen film debuted in March 1988 (see Holly Brear: *Inherit the Alamo*).

LEWIS, WILLIAM IRVINE
Virginia-born defender, 29, who died at the Alamo (see Bill Groneman: *Alamo Defenders*).

LIGHTFOOT, WILLIAM J.
Virginia-born artillerist, 25, who died at the Alamo (see Bill Groneman: *Alamo Defenders*).

Last Stand at the Alamo by Anthony M. DeSensi.

LILLEY, TIM
Ohio-based publisher of *The Big Trail*, a John Wayne films newsletter, and the editor/compiler of two books, *Campfire Conversations* (1992) and *Campfires Rekindled* (1994), that feature interviews with many of John Wayne's fellow actors and stuntmen from *The Alamo* (1960).

LINDLEY, JONATHAN
Alamo artillerist who probably hailed from Tennessee and died in the March 6, 1836, battle (see Thomas R. Lindley: "A Correct List of Alamo Patriots" in *The Alamo Journal*, #89, December 1993).

LINDLEY, THOMAS RICKS
Texas history researcher who heads Texian Army Investigations in Austin. Lindley has written a number of provocative articles for *The Alamo Journal* and has authored *To Fight the Mexican Eagle: The Ewings of the Texas Revolution*. His forthcoming volume on the Alamo is tentatively titled *Alamo Traces: Back Tracking the Historiography of the Texian Alamo*.

LINENTHAL, EDWARD TABOR
Author of 1991 book *Sacred Ground: Americans and Their Battlefields*, which features an assessment of the Alamo of history and popular culture.

LINN, WILLIAM
Maine-born defender, 16, who died at the Alamo (see "William Linn — Alamo Defender," *The Alamo Journal*, #101, June 1996).

LLEWELLYN, THOMAS
Texian infantry captain in Ben Milam's division during Siege and Battle of Béxar in 1835 (see Alwyn Barr: *Texans in Revolt*).

LOCKHART, BYRD
Virginia (or Missouri)-born Alamo courier, 54, who may have ridden to the mission-fortress with the Gonzales Ranging Company. Lockhart died in the town that bears his name in 1839 (see Bill Groneman: *Alamo Defenders*).

LONE STAR: A HISTORY OF TEXAS AND THE TEXANS

Epic 1968 work of noted Texas novelist and historian T. R. Fehrenbach. The 729-page work was reprinted in paperback in 1980. Of Crockett's death: "Mexican accounts say, probably accurately, that a few defenders vainly attempted to surrender. These, who may have included Crockett, were shot."

LONG, JEFF

Texas-based author who severely criticized the motives of the Alamo defenders in *Duel of Eagles* (1990). Of Crockett's death: "The Go Ahead Man quit. He did more than quit. He lied. He dodged. He denied his role in the fighting."

LONG, WALTER

Actor who played Santa Anna in *The Martyrs of the Alamo* in 1915 (see Frank Thompson: *Alamo Movies*).

LORD, WALTER

Best-selling author (*A Night To Remember, Day of Infamy*, etc.) who penned the highly-regarded 1961 volume *A Time To Stand*.

LOSOYA, TORIBIO

Tejano defender who participated in the December 1835 capture of Béxar and who died at the Battle of the Alamo. Losoya was honored with a life-sized bronze sculpture created by William Easley in 1986. Located on the Paseo del Alamo near Losoya Street in San Antonio, the sculpture was dedicated in a ceremony on November 30, 1986.

LOSOYA, JUAN

Noncombatant brother of Toribio Losoya, who survived the Battle of the Alamo (see Timothy M. Matovina: *The Alamo Remembered: Tejano Accounts and Perspectives*).

LOWMAN, SHEPARD C.

Student at Houston's Mirabeau B. Lamar High School who won the James Monroe Hill Texas History Essay Award in 1942 for "The Siege and Fall of the Alamo."

McCAFFERTY, EDWARD
Alamo lieutenant of unknown age who died at the Alamo (see Bill Groneman: *Alamo Defenders*).

McCARDLE, HENRY
Painter of *Dawn at the Alamo*, an 1883 work which not only depicts Crockett and Travis but also Robert Evans, who attempts to blow up some gunpowder (see Eric von Schmidt: "The Alamo Remembered — from a painter's point of view" in *Smithsonian*, March 1986).

McCOY, JESSE
Tennessee-born member of Gonzales Ranging Company, 32, who died at the Alamo (see Walter Lord: *A Time To Stand*).

McDOWELL, WILLIAM
Pennsylvania-born defender, 43, who died at the Alamo (see Walter Lord: *A Time To Stand*).

McGEE, JAMES
Irishman of unknown age who served in New Orleans Grays and died at the Alamo (see Bill Groneman: *Alamo Defenders*).

McGREGOR, JOHN
Scotsman, 27, whose spirited bagpipe playing cheered the Alamo defenders during the thirteen-day siege. McGregor, an artillery sergeant, died in the assault of March 6 (see Walter Lord: *A Time To Stand*).

McKINNEY, ROBERT
Tennessee-born defender, 27, who died at the Alamo (see Bill Groneman: *Alamo Defenders*).

McMULLEN, JOHN
President *pro tem* of the General Council and chair of committee which drew up a list of grievances on January 11, 1836, against Gov. Henry Smith, who had criticized the representative body for supporting a plan to invade Matamoros, Mexico (see Bob Boyd: *The Texas Revolution: A Day-by-Day Account*).

MAGNIFICENT BARBARIANS, THE
Bill and Marjorie Walraven's 1993 book (complete title: *The*

Magnificent Barbarians: Little Told Tales of the Texas Revolution) which highlights such topics as Alamo flags, Lorenzo De Zavala, and the Crockett death controversy, among others. The authors also supply an appendix that identifies U.S. Army deserters who joined the fight for Texas' independence.

MAIN, GEORGE WASHINGTON
Virginia-born Alamo lieutenant, 29, who died during the March 6 assault (see Bill Groneman: *Alamo Defenders*).

MALONE, WILLIAM T.
Georgia-born artillerist, 18, who died at the Alamo (see Bill Groneman: *Alamo Defenders*).

MAN OF CONQUEST
Republic Pictures film (1939) that focused on the life of Sam Houston (Richard Dix) and included a brief Alamo sequence featuring Victor Jory (Travis), Robert Armstrong (Bowie), and Robert Barratt (Crockett) (see Bruce Dettman: "Man of Conquest: Houston on Film" in *The Alamo Journal*, #87, July 1993).

MAN FROM THE ALAMO, THE
Universal-International film (1953) that focuses on the life of a ficticious Alamo defender, John Stroud, played by Glenn Ford, who leaves the mission-fortress during the siege in order to take care of the women and children of Oxbow, Texas. This Budd Boetticher-directed motion picture featured Arthur Space (Travis), Stuart Randalo (Bowie), and Trevor Bardette (Crockett) (see Frank Thompson: *Alamo Movies*).

MARSHALL, WILLIAM
Tennesesse-born defender, 28, who died at the Alamo (see Bill Groneman: *Alamo Defenders*).

MARTIN, ALBERT
Rhode Island-born Alamo courier who negotiated briefly with Col. Juan N. Almonte on February 23, 1836. Martin brought Travis' famous "Victory or Death" letter to Gonzales before returning to the Alamo, where he died on March 6 (see Walter Lord: *A Time To Stand*).

MARX ALAMO PLAYSETS
Boxed plastic 54mm playsets produced by Marx Toys in the 1950s featuring the Walt Disney trademark among several other generic models, including a miniature version called "Border Battle." One early model featured *Indians* attacking the Alamo!

MATOVINA, TIMOTHY M.
Author of the 1995 book *The Alamo Remembered: Tejano Accounts and Perspectives.*

MAVERICK, MARY ANN ADAMS
Alabamian who painted an 1838 watercolor of the Alamo chapel front and part of the Long Barracks, titled *The Old Church of San Antonio Valero* (see Mary A. and George M. Maverick: *Memoirs of Mary A. Maverick*).

MATAMOROS BATTALION
Veteran Mexican infantry unit under the command of Col. Jose Maria Romero which composed Santa Anna's third assault column of March 6 (see Albert Nofi: *The Alamo and the War for Texas Independence*).

MEISSNER, ALVIN R.
Designer of 1936 Texas Centennial three-cent postage stamp which featured the Alamo chapel and the images of Sam Houston and Stephen F. Austin.

MELTON, ELIEL
Georgia-born quartermaster, 38, who died at the Alamo (see Walter Lord: *A Time To Stand*).

"MEMORIES OF THE ALAMO"
A restrained ballad written by Anthony Pasqua, Michael Boldt, and William Pasqua. The song was perfomed inside the Alamo chapel by Anthony Pasqua and Michael Boldt on the night of March 5, 1995, at the inaugural ceremonial meeting of the Alamo Defenders Descendants Association (see Ralph R. Ortgega: "New Jersey Trio Put Alamo Memories to Music" in *Asbury Park Sunday Press*, March 26, 1995).

"MEXICAN SERGEANT'S RECOLLECTIONS OF THE ALAMO & SAN JACINTO, A"

Francisco Becerra's account of the Siege and Battle of the Alamo (the San Jacinto entries are lost) as told to ex-Texas Ranger John S. "Rip" Ford in 1875. Becerra claims to have been present when Travis and Crockett were killed together in the same room.

MEYERS, L. F.

Author of the 1896 publication *History, Battles and Fall of the Alamo.*

MICHENER, JAMES

Popular best-selling author (*The Bridges at Toko-Ri; Centennial; Hawaii;* and *Poland,* among many others) who penned *Texas* in 1985. The book was later made into the 1995 TV movie titled *James A. Michener's "Texas."* Michener describes Crockett's death in the following manner: ". . . a Mexican officer claimed that the last of the famous defenders to survive was Davy Crockett. 'He hid under a pile of women's clothes and begged and pleaded and wept when we trapped him. Said he would do anything if we spared him, but we shot him in contempt.' Unlikely, that."

MILAM, BENJAMIN RUSH

Welschman from Tennessee, 47, who initiated the Texian assault on Mexican-held San Antonio during Battle of Béxar in December 1835. Colonel Milam, who commanded the First Division (Francis W. Johnson led the other), was shot and killed on December 7 (see Alwyn Barr: *Texans in Revolt*).

MILLER, THOMAS R.

Tennessee-born member of the Gonzales Ranging Company, 41, who died at the Alamo (see Bill Groneman: *Alamo Defenders*).

MILLS, WILLIAM

Tennessee-born defender, 21, who died at the Alamo (see Bill Groneman: *Alamo Defenders*).

MILLSAPS, ISAAC

Mississippi-born member of Gonzales Ranging Company, 41, who died at the Alamo. A poignant letter allegedly penned by

Millsaps during the Alamo siege to his family was later determined to be a forgery (see Gregory Curtis: "Forgery Texas Style" in *Texas Monthly*, March 1989).

MISSIONS
Name of San Antonio-based minor league baseball team (AA Texas League, Western Division) in the Los Angeles Dodgers system which features the Alamo facade on its logo. The team plays in Municipal Stadium, which has an Alamo-shaped scoreboard in right field.

MITCHASSON, EDWARD F.
Virginia-born doctor, 30, who died at the Alamo (see Bill Groneman: *Alamo Defenders*).

MITCHELL, EDIN T.
Alamo defender, 30, who died during March 6 assault. Mitchell's brother, Dewarren, was executed during the Goliad Massacre (see Bill Groneman: *Alamo Defenders*).

MOFFITT, VIRGINIA MAY
Author of 1935 pamphlet, "Remember the Alamo!"

MONROE DEMOCRAT
New York state newspaper which heralded in a post-Battle of the Alamo headline on April 5, 1836, that: "Davy Crocket (sic) not dead." The newspaper noted: ". . . the report of the eccentric Davy Crockett is not true. He started (says the letter) on a hunting expedition to the Rocky Mountains, and then dropped down into Texas; but we expect him home early in the Spring."

MOORE, JOHN H.
Texian commander of Upper Division under Stephen F. Austin in November 1835. Colonel Moore had eight companies in his command (see Alwyn Barr: *Texans in Revolt: The Battle for San Antonio, 1835*).

MOORE, ROBERT B.
Virginia-born defender, 55, who came to Texas as a member of the New Orleans Grays and died at the Alamo (see Walter Lord: *A Time To Stand*).

MOORE, WILLIS A.
Twenty-eight-year-old cousin of Alamo defender Robert Moore. Both died during the March 6 assault (see Bill Groneman: *Alamo Defenders*).

MORALES, COL. JUAN
Mexican commander of the San Luis Potosi Battalion who led Santa Anna's fourth Alamo assault column of some 100 men on March 6 (see Stephen L. Hardin: *Texian Iliad*).

MORELOS BATTALION
Commanded by Nicholas Condelle, this Mexican unit was forced to surrender following the Battle of Béxar in December 1835 (see Stephen L. Hardin: *Texian Iliad*).

MORGAN, EMILY
Fictional character who was supposedly engaged in a romantic liaison with Santa Anna prior to Houston's attack at San Jacinto on April 21, 1836. A Ramada hotel (formerly the Medical Arts Building) that bears her name in San Antonio is situated across the street from the Alamo's north side (see Kent Biffle: "Yellow Rose Story Loses Its Bloom" in *Dallas Morning News*, November 17, 1985).

MORMAN, JOHN
Alamo defender not currently acknowledged as one who participated in the thirteen-day seige and battle (see Thomas R. Lindley: "A Correct List of Alamo Patriots" in *The Alamo Journal*, #89, December 1993).

MUNSON, JAMES R.
Alamo defender not currently acknowledged as one who participated in the thirteen-day siege and battle. An 1846 document lists thirty-three men as "Killed at the Alamo" or "With Travis." All the names can be found on other extant Alamo rosters except for seven. Of these men, five were at Goliad and two, William Harrell and James R. Munson, probably died at the Alamo (see Thomas R. Lindley: "A Correct List of Alamo Patriots" in *The Alamo Journal*, #89, December 1993).

MURPHY, KEITH
Author of 1979 children's book, *Battle of the Alamo*.

MUSSELMAN, ROBERT

Ohio-born sergeant, 31, (real name: F. Musselman) who died at the Alamo (see Thomas R. Lindley: "A Correct List of Alamo Patriots" in *The Alamo Journal*, #89, December 1993).

MUSSO, JOSEPH

James Bowie/Bowie Knife authority and creator of the 1962 painting *The Alamo: After The Fall.* Musso also created the panel art in San Antonio's Texas Adventure.™

MUSTER ROLLS OF THE TEXAS REVOLUTION

Daughters of the Republic of Texas-published volume that includes military muster rolls covering the 1835-1846 time period. The 1986 volume allows researchers to trace the service of various Alamo defenders and couriers.

MYERS, JOHN MYERS

Author of *The Alamo*, a 1948 volume about the famous 1836 siege and battle. Noted Myers in his conclusion: "The Alamo isn't a structure now; it is a symbol of valor in the minds of men. It can never fall again."

NAGASHINO CASTLE

Battle for this Japanese fortification in 1575 inspired Shigetka Shiga to donate a monument to the Alamo on November 6, 1914.

NAISH, J. CARROLL

Actor who played Santa Anna in *The Last Command* in 1955 (see Frank Thompson: *Alamo Movies*).

NAKED GUN, THE

Paramount film (full title: *The Naked Gun: from The Files of Police Squad*) directed by David Zucker, which includes several Alamo and David Crockett art and prop embellishments. For example, a painting of the Alamo chapel is featured on the bedroom wall of Lt. Frank Drebin's (Leslie Nielson) apartment and the Alamo Society is also acknowledged in the final credits (see *"The Naked Gun's* Alamo Touches" in *The Alamo Journal*, December 1988).

NAKED GUN 2 1/2

David Zucker's 1991 followup (full title: *The Naked Gun 2 1/2: The Smell of Fear*) to *The Naked Gun*. Like the first Paramount film, Zucker includes more Alamo images in this comedy, including a large reproduction of the Robert Onderdonk *Fall of the Alamo* painting on the staircase hallway wall of the "White House." Zucker makes a cameo appearance as David Crockett (along with Robert Weil as George Russel) in a SWAT-team shoot out. (see "More *Naked Gun 2 1/2* Alamo Touches" in *The Alamo Journal*, July 1991).

NAKED GUN 33 1/3

Paramount's third film (full title: *Naked Gun 33 1/3: The Final Insult*) in the *Naked Gun* trilogy. Co-producers David Zucker and Robert Weiss maintain Lt. Frank Drebin's (Leslie Nielson) affinity for Alamo and David Crockett interior decorating in this 1994 Paramount film directed by Peter Segal.

NAVA, ANDRES

Twenty-six-year-old Tejano in Seguin's cavalry company who died at the Alamo (see Walter Lord: *A Time To Stand*).

NAVARRO, GERTRUDIS

Tejano noncombatant, 15, who survived the Battle of the Alamo with her sister, Juana Navarro de Alsbury, and nephew, Alijo Perez, Jr. (see Bill Groneman: *Alamo Defenders*).

NAVARRO, JOSE JUAN SANCHEZ

Adjutant inspector of the Department of Nuevo Leon who made extensive detailed sketches of the Alamo in 1836 (see Craig Covner: "Before 1850: A New Look at the Alamo Through Art and Imagery" in *The Alamo Journal*, #70, March 1990).

NEGGAN, GEORGE

South Carolina-born member of Gonzales Ranging Company, 27, who died at the Alamo (see Bill Groneman: *Alamo Defenders*).

NEILL, JAMES CLINTON

Alamo commander following the Battle of Béxar. While commanding the Alamo, Lt. Col. Neill, who served as chief of Texas ordnance, and Jim Bowie agreed that the Alamo should not be abandoned, contrary to a discretionary suggestion made by Sam Houston to remove the artillery and destroy the mission-fortress. Neill, however, departed from the Alamo on February 11, 1836, for twenty days leave to take care of his ill family, leaving the garrison in the hands of joint commanders William B. Travis and Jim Bowie (see Stephen L. Hardin: "J.C. Neill: The Forgotten Alamo Commander" in *The Alamo Journal*, #66, May 1989).

NELSON, ANDREW M.

Tennessee-born defender, 27, who died at the Alamo (see Bill Groneman: *Alamo Defenders*).

NELSON, EDWARD

South Carolinian, 20, who died at the Alamo with his older brother, George (see Bill Groneman: *Alamo Defenders*).

NELSON, GEORGE

Texas-based artist who created the bronze relief Alamo compound that is situated on Alamo Plaza across from the Alamo chapel. The creation was formally unveiled during a public ceremony on April 21, 1986 (see "Bronze Relief Erected In Plaza" in *The Alamo Journal*, #51, July 1986).

NELSON, GEORGE

South Carolinian, 31, who died at the Alamo with his younger brother, Edward (see Bill Groneman: *Alamo Defenders*).

NOBLES, BENJAMIN F.

Lieutenant in Capt. Philip Dimmit's company which left the Alamo on February 23. Nobles later fought at the Battle of San Jacinto (see Bill Groneman: *Alamo Defenders*).

NOFI, ALBERT

New York-based military historian who authored *The Alamo and the Texas War for Independence* (1992). Of Crockett's death, Nofi says: ". . . it is probable that the story told by de la Péna (in which Crockett surrendered) is correct."

NORTON, FLETCHER
Actor who plated Santa Anna in *Davy Crockett and the Fall of the Alamo* in 1926 (see Frank Thompson: *Alamo Movies*).

NORTHCROSS, JAMES
Virginia-born artillerist, 32, who died at the Alamo (see Bill Groneman: *Alamo Defenders*).

NOWLAN, JAMES
Englishman, 27, who was wounded at the Battle of Béxar and died at the Alamo (see Bill Groneman: *Alamo Defenders*).

NUEVO LEON
Town in Mexico which supplied cavalrymen for two of seven mounted units stationed at the Alamo in 1835 (see Alwyn Barr: *Texans in Revolt: The Battle for San Antonio, 1835*).

OLMOS, EDWARD JAMES
Actor who played Santa Anna in *Seguin* in 1982 (see Frank Thompson: *Alamo Movies*).

ONDERDONK, ROBERT
Maryland-born painter of *Fall of the Alamo*, a 1903 commissioned work for Dallas businessman James T. DeShields, which prominently features Crockett swinging his rifle (see Eric von Schmidt: "The Alamo Remembered — from a painter's point of view" in *Smithsonian*, March 1986).

ORIGIN AND FALL OF THE ALAMO, MARCH 6, 1836
John Salmon "Rip" Ford's 1896 publication. Of Crockett's death: "Sergeant Becerra was of the opinion that the two last men killed were Travis and Colonel Crockett, though he admitted he did not know them personally and might be mistaken as to their identity."

OSBOURNE, OZZY
British heavy-metal singer who urinated on the Alamo Cenotaph on February 19, 1982, during a drunken sojourn on Alamo Plaza. Ten years later, Osbourne apologized to the Daughters of the Republic of Texas by donating $10,000 to the group (see "All in a Day's Work for the DRT" in *The Alamo Journal*, #83, September 1992).

OUR LIVING ALAMO
Mrs. S. J. Wright's 1937 book which traces the history of the famous mission-fortress. Of Crockett's death: "Davy Crockett, 'mighty hunter of the West,' died in the corner near the church, piles of slain about him."

OURY, WILLIAM SANDERS
Virginia-born courier, 18, who left the Alamo in late February. Oury later participated in the Battle of San Jacinto (see Bill Groneman: *Alamo Defenders*).

PADILLA, RUBEN
Actor who portrayed Santa Anna in *The Alamo* (1960) (see Don Clark and Christopher Andersen: *John Wayne's The Alamo*).

PAGAN, GEORGE
Veteran of the Battle of Béxar, 26, who died at the Alamo (see Bill Groneman: *Alamo Defenders*).

PAINE, SHEPERD
Master military sculptor who created *To The Last Man*, a limited 1986 edition pewter creation depicting a detailed look at the Battle of the Alamo.

PARKER, CHRISTOPHER ADAMS
Alamo private, 26, who died in the March 6 assault (see Bill Groneman: *Alamo Defenders*).

PARKER, FESS
Texas-born (August 16, 1924) actor who starred in the three-part Walt Disney production *Davy Crockett, King of the Wild Frontier,* during the 1954-55 TV season. The final episode, "Davy Crockett at the Alamo," aired on February 23, 1955. Parker appeared in a number of feature films and starred in *Daniel Boone,* a successful TV series in the 1960s. Following his acting career, Parker entered into the real estate and wine businesses in California. His celebrated wines feature a small coonskin cap on the labels. Parker wrote a column in *The Alamo Journal* from the late 1980s to the mid-1990s titled "Talkin' With Fess."

PARKS, WILLIAM
North Carolina-born veteran of the Battle of Béxar, 31, who died at the Alamo (see Bill Groneman: *Alamo Defenders*).

PARROT, T. L. F.
Artillery commander of some eighteen men in Col. James Bowie's Lower Division during the Battle of Béxar (see Alwyn Barr: *Texans in Revolt*).

PATTON, JACK
Illustrator of *Texas History Movies*, the 1926-27 comic strip about the history of Texas published in the *Dallas News*.

PATTON, WILLIAM HESTER
Kentucky-born Alamo courier, 28, who left the Alamo prior to the arrival of Santa Anna's forces on February 23, 1836. He had served as an infantry captain in Ben Milam's First Division during the Siege and Battle of Béxar in 1835 and later joined Houston at the Battle of San Jacinto (see Bill Groneman: *Alamo Defenders*).

PEACOCK, J. W.
Texian infantry company commander in Col. Francis W. Johnson's Second Division during the Siege and Battle of Béxar (see Alwyn Barr: *Texans in Revolt*).

PEE-WEE'S BIG ADVENTURE
Warner Bros. comedy (1985) starring Paul Rubens, who searches for his missing bicycle in the Alamo "basement." Although the Alamo tour sequence was actually filmed at California's San Fernando Mission, Rubens actually runs out of the front doors of the real Alamo chapel during one scene (see Frank Thompson: *Alamo Movies*).

PEREZ, ALEJO, JR.
Tejano child, eighteen-months, who survived the Battle of the Alamo (see Bill Groneman: *Alamo Defenders*).

PERRY, RICHARDSON
Texas-born artillerist, 19, who died at the Alamo (see Bill Groneman: *Alamo Defenders*).

PHILIP, CRAIG

Author of *Last Stands: Famous Battles Against the Odds*. The book includes a ten-page section on the Alamo.

PHIPPEN, GEORGE

Artist who created the drawings in *The Alamo*, the 1960 promotional souvenir book which accompanied the release of John Wayne's epic film of the same name.

POLLARD, AMOS

Massachusetts-born doctor, 32, who moved to Columbia, Texas, after practicing medicine in New York City from the late 1820s to 1834. Pollard died at the Alamo on March 6, 1836 (see Ronald H. Livingston: "The Texas Residency of Amos Pollard, " *The Alamo Journal*, #95, February 1995).

POTTER, R.M.

Author of *The Fall of the Alamo*, which was printed in 1860. Of Crockett's death, Potter noted: ". . . when he sallied to meet his fate in the face of the foe, (he) was shot down."

PRESIDIO LA BAHIA

Spanish-built fortress in Goliad commanded by Lt. Col. Franciso Sandoval which was seized by a small Texian force on October 10, 1835, under George M. Collingsworth. In early 1836 the fort was occupied by over four hundred Texian volunteers under Col. James W. Fannin. Following an unsuccessful march out of the fort on March 19 and a loss at the Battle of Coleto Creek, Fannin surrendered. On March 27, 1836, most of Fannin's men were executed (see Craig H. Roell: *Remember Goliad!: A History of La Bahia*).

PROCTER, BEN H.

Author of thirty-six-page booklet *The Battle of the Alamo* (1986). On Crockett's death, Procter cites the two major conflicting accounts ("taking a heavy toll of enemy soldiers" vs "he surrendered along with five other men").

RAGSDALE, CRYSTAL SASSE

Author of *Women and Children of the Alamo* (1994), which profiles such Alamo noncombatants as Ana Salazar de Esparza, Juana Navarro Pérez Alsbury, and Susanna Dickinson, among others.

RAY, FREDERIC
Author who wrote and illustrated the 1955 children's book *The Story of the Alamo.*

READ, OPIE
Author of 1900 fictional work *In the Alamo.*

READINGS ON THE ALAMO
John F. Rios' 1987 publication which includes selections from such Alamo commentators as Walter Lord, Reuben Potter, Eugene C. Barker, J. Frank Dobie, and Adina de Zavala, among others.

"REMEMBER THE ALAMO: MEXICAN AND TEXIAN MUSIC OF 1836"
Star Line Production audio cassette produced by Ray Herbeck, Jr., in 1989 that features contemporary music of the Texas Revolution performed on period instruments. Side "A" features such Texian tunes as "Come To The Bower" while Side "B" includes such Mexican melodies as "La Cachuca."

"REMEMBER THE ALAMO"
J. Bowers tune performed by Johnny Cash on the 1963 Columbia Records LP, *Ring of Fire: The Best of Johnny Cash.*

"REMEMBER THE ALAMO"
Mid-nineteenth century ballad that includes the lines "When on the wide-spread battle plain/The horse-man's hand can scarce restrain/His pampered steed that spurs the rein/Remember the Alamo!" (see Peter Stines: "The First Alamo Songs?" in *The Alamo Journal*, #58, November 1987)

"REMEMBER THE ALAMO"
Claude Rains' narrated 1960 album on Noble Records. The recording was designed and produced by Lyle Kenyon Engel and written by Michael Avallone.

"REMEMBER THE ALAMO"
Sonny Lester-produced 1967 album on True Action Adventure Records.

"REMEMBER THE ALAMO!"
Virginia May Moffitt's eighteen-page, 1935 pamphlet about the famous 1836 battle. The publication does not specifically mention the death of David Crockett.

REMEMBER THE ALAMO!
Robert Penn Warren's 1958 children's book in the Landmark history and biography series. Says Warren of Crockett's death: "Upon being hit, he seized his rifle in his left hand and leaped to the middle of the room for space to swing it. But he was now open for a Mexican volley, and fell."

"REMEMBER THE ALAMO"
Country music album performed by Donnie McCormick, Larry Bowie, and Tommy Carlisle. The LP included such tunes as "Men of the Alamo," "Santa Anna's Coming," and the title track.

REMEMBER THE ALAMO
Amelia Barr's 1888 fictional work about the famous mission-fortress. Chapter Fourteen deals with the "Fall of the Alamo." Barr described Crockett and Travis as two of six Alamo defenders who were "surrounded by Castrillon and his soldiers" and executed.

REMEMBER THE ALAMO
Edward S. Ellis' 1914 book about the Siege and Battle of the Alamo. Of Crockett's death: "Crockett made no sign, but General Castrillon, accepting his silence as submission, stopped the fighting and hurried the few steps to where Santa Anna, his swarthy face aflame with rage, stood watching the struggle. A volley closed the career of the last six of the Alamo garrison."

REMEMBER THE ALAMO!
Science fiction book penned in 1980 by Kevin D. Randle and Robert C. Cornett about thirty-three Vietnam War vets who take a time machine trip back to the Alamo in 1836 "with submachine guns and grenades, tear gas and Uzis."

"REMEMBER THE ALAMO" MUSEUM
Small but tasteful San Antonio multimedia museum which was

located across from the Alamo on Alamo Plaza in the early 1980s before closing in 1983.

REMEMBER GOLIAD!
Craig H. Roell's 1994 book (complete title: *Remember Goliad!: A History of La Bahia*) about the famous fortress and its role in the Texas Revolution. The sixty-page book, with twenty-five illustrations, is part of the Fred Rider Cotten Popular History Series.

"REMEMBERING THE ALAMO"
Title of impressive 1986 exhibit at San Antonio's Witte Museum that featured everything from Alamo collectibles and Davy Crockett's fiddle to ceramics, photographs, and Eric Von Schmidt's large canvas, *The Storming of the Alamo.*

RENDEZVOUS AT THE ALAMO
Virgil Baugh's 1960 book (complete title: *Rendezvous at the Alamo: Highlights in the Lives of Bowie, Crockett and Travis*) about the Alamo's three principal defenders. Baugh makes no specific mention of how Crockett died; however, he does mention where he died: ". . . in the west battery . . ."

"REVOLT IN TEXAS LEADER TO ITS INDEPENDENCE FROM MEXICO, 1835-1836, THE"
Booklet penned in 1993 by Terry Hooker of the South and Central American Military Historians Society, an organization which is based in Cottingham, North Humberside, England. Hooker states that he does not believe Crockett was one of the Alamo defenders who surrendered and was subsequently executed. The publication features illustrations of Mexican troops by C. A. Norman.

REYNOLDS, JOHN PURDY
Pennsylvania-born doctor, 29, who migrated to Texas with William McDowell. Reynolds served as an infantryman at the Alamo. Both Reynolds and McDowell died in the March 6 assault (see Walter Lord: *A Time To Stand*).

RICE, JAMES
Author and illustrator who penned the 1989 children's book *Texas Jack at the Alamo.*

RICHARDS, NORMAN
Connecticut-based writer who penned *The Story of the Alamo,* a book for young readers, in 1970.

RIO GRANDE
Town in Mexico which supplied cavalrymen for one of seven mounted units stationed at the Alamo in 1835 (see Alwyn Barr: *Texans in Revolt: The Battle for San Antonio, 1835*).

RIOS, JOHN F.
Editor of the 1987 publication *Readings on the Alamo*.

RIVERO, JULIAN
Actor who played Santa Anna in *Heroes of the Alamo* in 1937 (see Frank Thompson: *Alamo Movies*).

ROBERTS, THOMAS H.
Alamo defender of unknown age and origin who died in the March 6 assault (see Mary Ann Guerra: *Heroes of the Alamo and Goliad*).

ROBERTSON, JAMES WATERS
Tennessee-born defender, 24, who died at the Alamo (see Mary Ann Guerra: *Heroes of the Alamo and Goliad*).

ROBINSON, ISAAC
Scotsman, 28, who allegedly served as an Alamo artillerist and died in the March 6 assault. However, recent research suggests that Robinson may not have been at the Alamo (see Thomas Ricks Lindley: "A Correct List of Alamo Patriots" in *The Alamo Journal*, #89, December 1993).

ROELL, CRAIG. H.
Author of *Remember Goliad!: A History of La Bahia*, c. 1994, Roell examines the famous fortress within the historical context of its geographic location.

ROLLING STONES, THE
Veteran British band led by vocalist Mick Jagger and guitarist Keith Richards whose 1994 album, *Voodoo Lounge* (Virgin Records), featured an Alamo-inspired song, "Mean Disposition." The song included the lines: "I'm gonna go out and

stand my ground/Like Crockett at the Alamo/I'm gonna draw the line/One of us has got to go . . . "

ROMERO, JOSE MARIA
Mexican colonel in Santa Anna's command who led the third assault column of some four hundred men of the Jimenez and Matamoros Battalions against the Alamo on March 6, 1836 (see Albert Nofi: *The Alamo and the Texas War for Independence*).

ROSE, JAMES
Ohio-born defender, 31, who died at the Alamo. Susannah Dickinson made several documented comments about Rose in later years (see C. Richard King: *Susanna Dickinson —Messenger of the Alamo*).

ROSE, LOUIS "MOSES"
Frenchman, 50, who allegedly served with Napoleon Bonaparte and traveled to Texas in the 1820s. Rose "departed" from the Alamo prior to the March 6 battle and remained for a time with the Zuber family. According to William Zuber in 1873, Rose had told him that William B. Travis drew a line in the dirt asking the men to stay and fight with him (see Walter Lord: *A Time To Stand*).

ROSENFIELD, JOHN JR.
Author of *Texas History Movies*, the 1926-27 comic strip about the history of Texas published in the *Dallas News*.

ROSENTHAL, PHIL
Co-author with Bill Groneman of *Roll Call at the Alamo*, author of *Alamo Soldiers,* and founder of Alamo International (1980-1986). Rosenthal edited the Alamo International newsletters, *Alamo II* (from 1980-1982) and *The Alamo News* (1982-1984).

"RUNAWAY SCRAPE"
The departure of Texian familes in Gonzales and the subsequent retreat of Houston's army eastward to the Colorado River following news of the Alamo's fall (see Stephen L. Hardin: *Texian Iliad*).

RUSK, JACKSON J.
Irishman of unknown age who died at the Alamo (see Mary Ann Guerra: *Heroes of the Alamo and Goliad*).

RUSK, THOMAS J.
Company commander in James Bowie's division during the Battle of Béxar in 1835. Rusk later became the revolutionary republic's secretary of war and later participated in the Battle of San Jacinto (see Alwyn Barr: *Texans in Revolt*).

RUTHERFORD, JOSEPH
Kentucky-born artillerist, 38, who died at the Alamo (see the Daughters of the Republic of Texas: *The Alamo Long Barrack Museum*).

RYAN, ISAAC
Louisiana-born defender, 31, who died at the Alamo (see Daughters of the Republic of Texas: *The Alamo Long Barrack Museum*).

SABINE RIVER
River that separates Texas from Louisiana. Prior to 1835 it was the boundary between Mexico and the United States. Two U.S. military bases, Fort Jessup and Camp Sabine, were established on the river's east bank by Gen. Edmund P. Gaines prior to the Texas Revolution (see Stephen L. Hardin: *Texian Iliad*).

SACRED GROUND: AMERICANS AND THEIR BATTLEFIELDS
Edward Taylor Linenthal's 1991 book about the Alamo and other battlefield sites such as Pearl Harbor, Gettysburg, and the Little Big Horn, among others. According to the author, the identified places are frequently associated with religious themes that promote myth and ritual.

SAN ANTONIO
Warner Brothers' 1945 film starring Errol Flynn, in which a full-scale Alamo chapel front was contructed on the studio's Calabasa Ranch lot in California. Flynn's character, Clay Hardin, has a six-gun shootout inside the "Alamo" during the film's finale.

SAN ANTONIO LIVING HISTORY ASSOCIATION
Living history organization formed in the summer of 1986 by Gary Foreman and Robert Carrier during a break in the filming of *Houston: The Legend of Texas* at Alamo Village in Brackettville, Texas. The group has sponsored numerous living history events which recreate the life and times of the Texas Revolution, including annual March 6 dawn ceremonies on Alamo Plaza (see Holly Brear: *Inherit the Alamo*).

SANDERS, DAVID
Painter of *The Survivor* (1988), which depicts a resting longhorn with the Alamo and the last of the departing Mexican cavalry in the background (see *Kaleidoscope, The Guide to Austin*, Fall 1988).

SANDINO, ENRIQUE
Actor who played Santa Anna in *Alamo . . . The Price of Freedom* in 1988 (see Frank Thompson: *Alamo Movies*).

SANDOR, STEVE
Rugged actor who played James Bowie in the IMAX film *Alamo . . . The Price of Freedom* (see Frank Thompson: *Alamo Movies*).

SANTA ANNA, ANTONIO LOPEZ
President of Mexico who abolished Constitution of 1824 and led the Mexican Army into Texas to suppress the revolution. Santa Anna (complete name: Antonio Lopez de Santa Anna Perez de Lebron), who initiated the siege of the Alamo on February 23, 1836, was defeated by Texian forces under Sam Houston at San Jacinto on April 21, 1836 (see Albert Nofi: *The Alamo and the Texas War for Independence*).

SANTA ANNA'S CAMPAIGN AGAINST TEXAS, 1835-1836
Richard G. Santos' 1968 volume about the Texas revolution. The author emphasizes Mexican primary sources in his publication. Of Crockett's death: "According to colonels de la Peña, Sanchez Navarro, Almonte and Urriza, David Crockett, a well-known naturalist from North America, was among the captured. Santa Anna severely reprimanded Castrillon for sparing their lives and ordered the Texans to be killed."

Enrique Sandino as Santa Anna with his staff in a scene from Alamo . . . The Price of Freedom. Sponsored by Luby's. © 1996 River Theatre.

SANTOS, RICHARD G.
Former chairman of the Béxar County Historical Commission and author of the 1968 book *Santa Anna's Campaign Against Texas, 1835-1836*. Santos suggested that the Alamo defenders numbered over two hundred-fifty and that Santa Anna's assault force numbered no more than fifteen hundred men.

SAUCEDO, TRINIDAD
Female Tejano, 27, who survived the Battle of the Alamo (see Daughters of the Republic of Texas: *The Alamo Long Barrack Museum*).

SCHNEIDER, JOHN
Actor who played Davy Crockett in the 1995 TV movie *James A. Michener's "Texas."*

SCURLOCK, MIAL
North Carolina defender (either 27 or 33) who settled in San Augustine, Texas, and died at the Alamo. Some evidence suggests that Scurlock may have been stationed at Goliad instead (see Bill Groneman: *Alamo Defenders*).

SECOND REINFORCEMENT THEORY
Idea which sugggests that a group of reinforcements joined the Alamo defenders in addition to the Gonzales Ranging Company, which had joined the garrison after the siege began on February 23, 1836. According to recent research suggested by Thomas R. Lindley of Texian Army Investigations, the second reinforcement included Stephen Dennison, Edward McCafferty, John W. Thompson, Edward F. Mitchusson, William Moore, Thomas H. Roberts, M. B. Clark, T. P. Hutchinson, James Holloway, Henry Thomas, Edwin Mitchell, Conrad Eigenauer, Henry Courtman, and Mial Scurlock. These men probably died at the Alamo, except for Mitchell and Scurlock, who may have been stationed at Goliad since both had brothers there (see Thomas R. Lindley: "A Correct List of Alamo Patriots" in *The Alamo Journal*, #89, December 1993).

SEGUIN
PBS "American Playhouse" series production (1982) of Juan

Seguin's life. The Jesus Trevino film, which was shot at Alamo Village in Brackettville, Texas, the site of John Wayne's *The Alamo*, features a brief Alamo segment that includes the execution of several defenders following the battle (see Frank Thompson: *Alamo Movies*).

SEGUIN, JUAN NEPOMUCENO
San Antonio de Béxar-born cavalry commander, 29, who acted

Cavalryman in Juan Seguin's Company. Illustration by Gary Zaboly.

as a courier for William B. Travis during the Siege of the Alamo. Seguin protected Houston's retreating army during the "Runaway Scrape" and participated at the Battle of San Jacinto. In 1841 Seguin was elected the mayor of San Antonio but proved unpopular to the recent immigrants who came from the United States. He departed Texas for Mexico in 1842 and experienced several tumultuous years before returning to his birthplace (see Jack Jackson: *Los Tejanos*).

SEWELL, MARCUS
Englishman, 31, member of Gonzales Ranging Company who died at the Alamo (see Daughters of the Republic of Texas: *The Alamo Long Barrack Museum*).

SHACKELFORD, JACK
Captain of Alabama Red Rovers, a volunteer Anglo unit attached to Fannin's Goliad command. Shackelford, a doctor, was spared by the Mexicans during the March 27, 1836, massacre at Goliad (see Stephen L. Hardin: *Texian Iliad*).

SHACKFORD, JAMES ATKINS
Author of *David Crockett: The Man and the Legend* (1956). Of Crockett's death at the Alamo, Shackford wrote: ". . . David's death was quite undramatic, that he was one of the first to fall, and that he died unharmed."

SHEPARD, SETH
Author of the 1889 publication *The Fall of the Alamo: An Oration*.

SHIELD, MASON
Georgia-born artillerist, 25, who died at the Alamo (see Phil Rosenthal and Bill Groneman: *Roll Call at the Alamo*).

SHIGA, SHIGETKA
Japanese historian from Okazaki who donated a granite monument to the Alamo defenders on November 6, 1914. Shiga was inspired by the parallels between the Alamo of 1836 and a Japanese battle for Nagashino Castle in 1575.

SHOW, GRANT
Actor who played William Barret Travis in the 1995 TV movie *James A. Michener's "Texas."*

SIEGE AND FALL OF THE ALAMO, THE

A 1914 silent motion picture that is considered to be the first feature-length Alamo film. Shot in San Antonio, it was released on June 1, 1914, just weeks after President Woodrow Wilson sent U.S. Marines to take control of Vera Cruz, Mexico (see Frank Thompson: *Alamo Movies*).

"SIEGE AND FALL OF THE ALAMO, THE"

Mirabeau B. Lamar High School (Houston) student Shepard C. Lowman's 1942 award-winning James Monroe Hill Texas History Essay. Of Crockett's death: "Crockett and his Tennessee boys make their last stand by the pickett wall that runs from the barracks to the chapel."

SIEGE AND TAKING OF THE ALAMO, THE

Gen. Miguel A. Sanchez Lamego-authored 1968 book (translated by Consuelo Velasco) about Santa Anna's Army of Operations at the Siege and Battle of the Alamo. The book compares and contrasts three versions of Crockett's death.

SIMMONS, CLEVELAND KINLOCH

South Carolina-born lieutenant in Capt. John Forsyth's cavalry company who died at the Alamo (see Bill Groneman: *Alamo Defenders*).

SMITH, ANDREW H.

Tennessee defender, 21, who may have deserted from Capt. John Forsyth's cavalry company. Still, he is listed in the Alamo as a March 6, 1836, fatality (see Bill Groneman: *Alamo Defenders*).

SMITH, CHARLES S.

Maryland-born artillerist, 30, who died at the Alamo (see Daughters of the Republic of Texas: *The Alamo Long Barrack Museum*).

SMITH, ERASTUS "DEAF"

New York-born and Mississippi-raised scout of the Texas Revolution. Despite a drastic loss of hearing, Smith was an exceptional rider and superior shooter. He scouted the Concepcion region for Jame Bowie, participated in the Battle of Béxar, and served with Houston at Gonzales in early March 1836. Following the fall of the Alamo, Smith was one of the scouts who found Susannah and Angelina Dickinson. He later participated in the Battle of San Jacinto (see Bob Boyd: *The Texas Revolution: A Day-by-Day Account*).

SMITH, JOHN WILLIAM
Virginia-born Alamo courier, 44, who was later elected mayor of San Antonio (see Stephen L. Hardin: *Texian Iliad*).

SMITHER, LAUNCELOT
Alabama-born Alamo courier, 23, who left the Alamo following the arrival of Santa Anna's army on the afternoon of February 23, 1836 (see Walter Lord: *A Time To Stand*).

SMU MUSTANG
Official quarterly publication of the Southern Methodist University alumni which featured a cover story, "A Tale of Two Alamos," written by Dr. Paul Andrew Hutton in its Spring 1986 issue. The article, replete with photos, comic art, and drawings, was actually taken from Hutton's introduction to *Alamo Images: Changing Perceptions of a Texas Experience*.

SONS OF THE REPUBLIC OF TEXAS (SRT)
Fraternal organization formed in 1922 with hereditary requirements somewhat similar to the Daughters of the Republic of Texas. The SRT promotes researching Texas history and commemorates the Siege and Battle of the Alamo with an annual program titled "This Hallowed Ground" (see Holly Brear: *Inherit the Alamo*).

"SONGS FOR THE ALAMO"
Stage Door Productions' 1994 LP of fourteen tracks performed by various artists including "Never, Never Forget," "Crockett's Dance," and "The Green Leaves of Summer," sung by the Brothers Four.

SOWELL, ANDREW JACKSON
Tennessee-born Alamo courier, 20, who left the Alamo prior to the March 6 assault (see Bill Groneman: *Alamo Defenders*).

SPENCER, LEE

Member of the Daughters of the Republic of Texas and first president (1995) of the Alamo Defenders Descendants Association. She chaired the organization's first Rememberance Ceremony inside the Alamo chapel on March 5, 1995.

"SPIRIT OF THE ALAMO, THE"

Promotional video documentary-entertainment special on John Wayne's *The Alamo* which aired on ABC-TV on November 14, 1960. The program not only featured the principal cast members but former U.S. Vice President John Nance Garner, historian J. Frank Dobie, novelist Lon Tinkle, and rancher James T. "Happy" Shahan (see Donald Clark and Christopher Andersen: *John Wayne's The Alamo*).

SPRATT, WILLIAM

Alamo defender not currently aknowledged as one who participated in the thirteen-day siege and battle (see Thomas R. Lindley: "A Correct List of Alamo Patriots" in *The Alamo Journal, #89*, December 1993).

STAR OF THE ALAMO, THE

Willis Vernon-Cole's 1926 fictional work of the famous siege and battle. Of Crockett's death: "Uriah and Crockett clubbing muskets, piled the ground before the altar with dead. Crockett fell."

STARR, RICHARD

Englishman, 25, who died at the Alamo (see Daughters of the Republic of Texas: *The Alamo Long Barrack Museum*).

STEINBECK, JOHN

Author best known for *The Grapes of Wrath* who proposed an Alamo story line to film producer Jules Buck in 1949. Steinbeck's idea, which never even reached the pre-production stage, featured Santa Anna as a hero of sorts (see "Alamo Film Idea From The 40s" in *The Alamo Journal, #81*, May 1992).

STEWART, JAMES E.

Englishman, 28, who died at the Alamo (see Daughters of the Republic of Texas: *The Alamo Long Barrack Museum*).

STOCKTON, RICHARD L.

Virginia-born Alamo defender, 19, who died in the March 6 assault (see Daughters of the Republic of Texas: *The Alamo Long Barrack Museum*).

STORMING OF THE ALAMO

Simon Kerl's 1868 publication on the famous siege and battle. The book does not mention any specific reference to David Crockett's death.

STORIES BEHIND THE SCENES OF THE GREAT FILM EPICS, THE

Mike Munn's 1982 volume which states: "Regardless of (John) Wayne's Oscar-winning *True Grit*, *The Alamo* remains his finest achievement and long after his death it will stand as a monument to this great star."

"STORY OF THE ALAMO, THE"

J. C. Butterfield's 1913 pamphlet about the famous siege and battle.

STORY OF THE ALAMO, THE

Arie M. Claiborne's 1901 book. Of Crockett's death: "Crockett too fell early in the fight, but he left near him a little mound of the dead that he had slain."

STORY OF THE ALAMO, THE

Illustrator and author Frederic Ray created this 1955 book for young readers. Of Crockett's death, Ray wrote: "Crockett and his Tennessean riflemen fell in the area fronting the chapel, surrounded by the bodies of the Mexicans they had slain. . . ."

STORY OF THE ALAMO, THE

Author Norman Richards wrote this 1970 children's book that featured the illustrations of Tom Dunnington. *The Story of the Alamo* is part of the historical "Cornerstones of Freedom" series. Of Crockett's death, Richards wrote: "Then Davy Crockett fell dead, surrounded by enemy dead."

"STOUT AND HIGH"

Monte Warden tribute song about the walls of the Alamo performed in a 1988 A&M Records single by country music artists the Wagoneers. The song was also the title track of the group's debut LP (see Larry Monroe: "Austin Artists Score High During Past Year" in *Austin Weekly*, January 4, 1989).

SUMMERLIN, A. SPAIN
Tennessee born Alamo defender, 19, who died in the March 6 assault (see Bill Groneman: *Alamo Defenders*).

SUMMERS, WILLIAM E.
Tennessee-born member of Gonzales Ranging Company, 24, who was killed at the Alamo (see Bill Groneman: *Alamo Defenders*).

SUSANNA OF THE ALAMO
John Jakes' 1986 children's book about two Alamo non-combatants: Susanna Dickinson and her daughter, Angelina. Paul Bacon provided the illustrations for the book.

SUTHERLAND, DR. JOHN
Alleged Alamo courier, 43, who supposedly detected the advance units of Santa Anna's cavalry outside of San Antonio de Béxar on February 23, 1836. Sutherland later that day left the Alamo for Gonzales, which later contributed a small relief column, the so-called Gonzales 32. Following the Texas Revolution, Sutherland practiced medicine in Egypt, Texas. Recent research, however, suggests that Sutherland may have embellished his role in the Texas Revolution to take advantage of land grant opportunities (see Bill Groneman: *Alamo Defenders*).

SUTHERLAND, WILLIAM DePRIEST
Teenager, 17, Alamo defender and nephew of Dr. John Sutherland. He was killed at the Alamo (see Walter Lord: *A Time To Stand*).

SWISHER, JAMES G.
Texian infantry company commander in Col. Francis W. Johnson's Second Division during the Battle of Béxar in 1835. Swisher previously served as a company commander in Jim Bowie's Lower Division (see Alwyn Barr: *Texans in Revolt*).

TALL MEN WITH LONG RIFLES
James T. DeShields' 1935 volume about the Texas Revolution based on the recollections of participant Creed Taylor, who died in 1906. Of Crockett's death: "(Crockett) was killed in a room of the mission. A corporal ordered the passage cleared of those who were being pressed forward, a volley was fired almost point blank and the last defender of the Alamo fell forward — dead."

TAMAULIPAS
Town in Mexico which supplied cavalrymen for one of seven mounted units stationed at the Alamo in 1835 (see Alwyn Barr: *Texans in Revolt: The Battle for San Antonio, 1835*).

TAYLOR, EDWARD
Tennessee-born Alamo defender, 21, who was killed at the Alamo with his brothers, George and James (see Walter Lord: *A Time To Stand*).

TAYLOR, GEORGE
Tennessee-born Alamo defender, 20, who was killed at the Alamo with his brothers, Edward and James (see Walter Lord: *A Time To Stand*).

TAYLOR, JAMES
Tennessee-born Alamo defender, 22, who was killed at the Alamo with his brothers, Edward and George (see Walter Lord: *A Time To Stand*).

TAYLOR, WILLIAM
Tennessee-born Alamo defender, 37, who was killed at the Alamo (see Daughters of the Republic of Texas: *The Alamo Long Barrack Museum*).

TELEGRAPH AND TEXAS REGISTER
Newspaper published by Gail Borden, Jr., Tom Borden, and Josephine Baker in San Felipe. The March 24, 1836, issue printed an article, "More Particular Respecting The Fall Of The Alamo," and listed the known Texian casualties (see Walter Lord: *A Time To Stand*).

TEMPERED BLADE
Monte Barrett's 1946 fictional tale of Jim Bowie. Of Crockett's death: "When his gun was finally engulfed Crockett went down defending it with his clubbed rifle."

TEMPLETON, R. L.
Author of 1975 children's book, *Cannon Boy of the Alamo*, about William P. King, the Alamo's youngest defender. He also penned the 1976 fictional work, *Alamo Soldier: The Story of Peaceful Mitchell.* According to the author's introduction, Mitchell was "the only man in the Alamo who didn't want to kill, didn't believe in violence, or the taking of a life."

TENNESSEE
Volunteer state provided more native sons to the defense of the Alamo (31) than any other state or country. The state's most celebrated defender was David Crockett (see Daughters of the Republic of Texas: *The Alamo Long Barrack Museum*).

TENNESSEE MOUNTED VOLUNTEERS
Military unit commanded by Capt. William B. Harrison and sworn into service on January 14, 1836, at Nacogdoches. The unit, which arrived in San Antonio de Béxar on February 8 or 9, 1836, included David Crockett (see Walter Lord: *A Time To Stand*).

TESORO DEL ALAMO PRESERVATION SOCIETY
Texas-based non-profit organization devoted to raising funds for the 1994-95 Lost Wells Project on Alamo Plaza. The archaeologists involved in the project were unable to locate a well allegedly dug by the Alamo defenders in 1836 but uncovered various items from an early Native American food preparation site.

TEXAS GLORY: AN EPIC OF THE ALAMO
Robert Vaughan's 1996 fictional novel about the Siege and Battle of the Alamo. Of Crockett's death: "Then Sam saw a Mexican lieutenant come up behind Crockett and slash him just above the eye with a ferocious blow from his sword."

"TEXAS HISTORY MOVIES"
Comic strip series on Texas history printed in *Dallas News* in 1926-27. The strip, an idea of E. B. Doran, the director of news and telegraph for the *Dallas News* and the *Dallas Journal*, fea-

Tennessee Mounted Volunteer. Illustration by Gary Zaboly.

tured the text of John Rosenfield, Jr., and the illustrations of Jack Patton. The strip covered Texas from the 1490s to the late 1920s. Of Crockett's death: "Crockett was found dead near the south wall."

TEXAS IN REVOLT
Collection of contemporary newspaper articles (*New Orleans Bee, Troy Daily Whig, Louisiana Advertiser,* etc.) describing the Fall of the Alamo and the Battle of San Jacinto, compiled by Jerry J. Gaddy in 1973. The book is augmented by reproductions of several tempera paintings of the events by J. Hefter.

TEXAS JACK AT THE ALAMO
Lively 1989 children's book written and illustrated by James Rice that tells the story of the Alamo through the eyes of an eyewitness *jackrabbit*! Of Crockett's death: "Davy Crockett killed eight Mexicans and wounded several more with his clubbed rifle before he was surrounded and killed."

TEXAS LANDMARKS ASSOCIATION
Organization founded by Adina De Zavala in 1913. The group installed a marker in 1917 on East Commerce Street in San Antonio, Texas, which marked the site of one of the funeral pyres which had burned the bodies of the Alamo defenders. A new marker was installed on the site during a special presentation on March 6, 1995.

TEXAS REPUBLICAN
Newspaper published by Frank C. Gray, which published early acounts of the Alamo's siege, including Travis' famous "Victory or Death" letter of February 24, 1836, before ceasing publication on March 2, 1836 (see Bill and Marjorie K. Walraven: *The Magnificent Barbarians: Little Told Tales of the Texas Revolution*).

TEXAS REVOLUTION, THE
William C. Binkley's 1952 book, essentially a collection of four essays the Vanderbilt University History Department chairman delivered at Louisiana State University.

TEXAS REVOLUTION OF 1836, THE
Privately-printed book written by Roger Borreal in 1989

(complete title: *The Texas Revolution of 1836: A Concise Historical Perspective Based on Original Sources*). Of Crockett's death, the author states that "it has been proven beyond a doubt by the accounts of the actual participants that Crockett was one of six or seven Anglos to have surrendered after being found hiding in the low barracks."

TEXIAN
Term used to describe those settlers of Texas prior to statehood (1845), especially during the Texas Revolution (1835-36) and Texas Republic (1836-1845) years. Similar contemporary terms included "Texonians," "Texasians," "Coahi-Texans," "Béxarians" and "Texans" (see William Chemerka: "A Texan by any Other Name" in *The Alamo Journal*, #54, February 1987).

TEXIAN ILIAD: A MILITARY HISTORY OF THE TEXAS REVOLUTION
Stephen L. Hardin's excellent 1994 military history of the Texas Revolution. Augmented with illustrations by Gary Zaboly, *Texian Iliad* traces the revolution from its pre-1835 origins to the Battle of San Jacinto in 1836. The book, which won the 1995 Kate Broocks Bates Award, got its title from an 1839 description by French observer Frederic Gaillardet.

13TH DAY OF GLORY, THE
Buckskinner artist Doug Prine's 1984 painting of the Battle of the Alamo. The Texas artist embellished his Alamo defenders with a mountain man-like look as the defenders struggle with advancing Mexican soldiers in this detailed, though fanciful, work.

THOMAS, B. ARCHER M.
Kentucky-born Alamo defender, 18, who was killed during the March 6 assault (see Daughters of the Republic of Texas: *The Alamo Long Barrack Museum*).

THOMAS, HENRY
Alamo defender, 25, who was born in Germany and was killed in the March 6, 1836, assault (see Daughters of the Republic of Texas: *The Alamo Long Barrack Museum*).

THOMPSON, JESSE G.

Alamo defender on current roster who may not have been a participant in the famous thirteen-day 1836 siege (see Thomas Ricks Lindley: "A Correct List of Alamo Patriots" in *The Alamo Journal*, #89, December 1993).

THERMOPYLAE

Ancient battle fought between the Spartans and Persians in 480 B.C., in which the overwhelmed Spartan force, under King Leonidas, died to a man. On March 26, 1836, the town of Nacogdoches, Texas, issued a proclamation that compared Thermopylae to the Alamo. Years later, an inscription on the east front of the first Alamo monument erected in Austin read: "Thermopylae had her messenger of defeat, but the Alamo had none" (see A. Garland Adair and M. H. Crockett, eds.: *Heroes of the Alamo*).

THOMSON, JOHN W.

North Carolina-born Alamo defender, 29, who died in the March 6, 1836, assault (see Bill Groneman: *Alamo Defenders*).

THURSTON, JOHN M.

Pennsylvania-born Alamo officer (a second lieutenant of cavalry following his status as a first lieutenant in Louisville Volunteers), 26, who was killed during the March 6 battle (see Thomas R. Lindley: "A Correct List of Alamo Patriots" in *The Alamo Journal* #89, December 1993).

"TIME TUNNEL, THE"

Quirky ABC-TV sci-fi series which aired "The Alamo" episode on December 9, 1966, about a pair of time travelers who arrive at the Shrine of Texas Liberty on March 6, 1836 (see Frank Thompson: *Alamo Movies*).

TINKLE, LON

SMU professor of French and Comparative Literature who penned *13 Days To Glory* in 1958. His book was the basis of a 1987 NBC-TV movie, *The Alamo: 13 Days To Glory* (see Frank Thompson: *Alamo Movies*).

TOBEY, KENNETH
Character actor who played Jim Bowie in Walt Disney's *Davy Crockett, King of the Wild Frontier* (see Frank Thompson: *Alamo Movies*).

TO FIGHT THE MEXICAN EAGLE
Thomas R. Lindley-authored 1993 narrative (complete title: *To Fight the Mexican Eagle: The Ewings of the Texas Revolution*) about the family of Alamo defender James Lee Ewing.

TODISH, TIM J.
Author of 1997 volume *Alamo Sourcebook, 1836*.

TO THE LAST MAN
Sculptor Sheperd Paine's 1986 pewter creation for the Franklin Mint in which ten Alamo combatants are featured, including the figures of Davy Crockett and William B. Travis. The $750 sculpture, which measured approximately thirteen inches high and thirteen inches long, was issued in a limited edition of 4,500 copies.

TOLUCA BATTALION
Veteran infantry unit under Col. Francisco Duque which scaled the Alamo's North Wall during the pre-dawn March 6, 1836, assault.

TRAMMEL, BURKE
Irish artillerist, 26, who was killed at the Alamo (see Daughters of the Republic of Texas: *The Alamo Long Barrack Museum*).

TRAVIS, WILLIAM BARRET
South Carolina-born commander of the Alamo, 26, who originally shared command with James Bowie. During the thirteen-day siege, Travis penned a series of dramatic letters requesting help from various outposts. His most memorable letter (February 24, 1836) states, in part: "I am determined to sustain myself as long as possible & die like a soldier who never forgets what is due his own honor & that of his country. VICTORY or DEATH." Travis may have been one of the first Alamo defenders to be killed in the March 6 battle (see Stephen L. Hardin: "A Volley from the Darkness: Sources Re-

"El Cuchillo." A Toluca Battalion Rifleman examines Jim Bowie's famous knife after the Battle. Illustration by Gary Zaboly.

garding the Death of William Barret Travis" in *The Alamo Journal*, #59, December 1987).

"TRAVIS"

A 1991 Grace Productions Corporation video production about a modern girl (Holley Vaughn) who travels back in time to see William Barret Travis (Benton Jennings) at the Alamo.

TUMLINSON, GEORGE W.

Missouri-born artillerist, 22, who was killed at the Alamo (see Daughters of the Republic of Texas: *The Alamo Long Barrack Museum*).

TWO SIEGES OF THE ALAMO

Robert Edmond Alter's 1965 children's book about the famous siege and battle. Of Crockett's death: "The six men who surrendered came from the low barracks in the Plaza, and they were executed on the spot. But Mrs. Dickinson said that the first thing she saw when she came from the church was Crockett's body. So — if she saw his body in the chapel yard, and if the six who surrendered were killed in the Plaza, how did Crockett's body span the distance between the two points, and why? Sergeant Felix Nuñez (from whom we learn of the Tennessean who fought alone with his back to the corral wall) implies that this one American woodsman was indeed the mighty Crockett."

TYLEE, JAMES

New York-born Alamo defender who was killed at the Alamo (see Daughters of the Republic of Texas: *The Alamo Long Barrack Museum*).

UNDER SIX FLAGS

An Alamo film which only made it to preproduction in the early 1930s. The production company, Texas Pictures Inc., was headed by Clara Driscoll Sevier, who helped purchase the Alamo with her own money after the property was put up for sale by Hugo & Schmeltzer in 1903 (see Frank Thompson: *Alamo Movies*).

UGARTECHEA, DOMINGO DE

Mexican commander of San Antonio de Béxar in 1835.

Colonel Ugartechea sent a military unit under Lt. Francisco Castenada to Gonzales to retrieve the town's cannon, a bronze six-pounder, in what became the first military conflict of the Texas Revolution on October 2, 1835 (see Bob Boyd: *The Texas Revolution: A Day-by-Day Account*).

URREA, JUAN JOSE
Mexican brigadier general who commanded independent division which won victories over Texian forces at San Patricio, Refugio, Goliad, and Coleto Creek. A frequent critic of Santa Anna, Urrea refused to execute all the Goliad prisoners on March 27, 1836 (see Albert Nofi: *The Alamo and the Texas War for Independence*).

VENABLE, CLARKE
Author of 1929 fictional work *All the Brave Rifles* about the Siege and Battle of the Alamo.

VERAMENDI HOUSE
San Antonio home of Vice Governor Juan Martin Veramendi, whose daughter, Ursula, married Jim Bowie. The yard of the house became one of Santa Anna's artillery positions during the Siege of the Alamo (see Walter Lord: *A Time To Stand*).

VERNON-COLE, WILLIS
Author of 1926 fictional work, *The Star of the Alamo.*

"VICTORY OR DEATH"
Concluding statement that punctuated several of the letters that Alamo commander William Barret Travis wrote during the thirteen-day 1836 siege. Travis' famous letter of February 24 ends with these words underlined three times (see David Nevin: *The Texans*).

VICTORY OR DEATH
Living history socio-drama penned by Jack Edmondson and sponsored by the San Antonio Living History Association each March 6 on Alamo Plaza that ends in a tableaux-like setting of battling Texians and Mexicans (see Holly Brear: *Inherit the Alamo*).

"VICTORY OR DEATH"
First Alamo CD-ROM that features animation, maps,

weapons demonstrations, and assorted interactive games and puzzles. The 1995 production features contributions from various actors including Stacy Keach, who played Sam Houston in *James Michener's "Texas."*

VILLA DE BEXAR

Village founded on May 5, 1718, near San Pedro Springs and named for the Duke of Béxar, the brother of the Marquis de Valero, the viceroy of Mexico in the Spanish empire. Four days earlier, the mission San Antonio de Valero was founded, the first mission in what is now San Antonio. A presidio was also founded on May 5, 1718, but it later moved to Military Plaza in 1722.

VIVA MAX

Jerry Paris-directed 1969 comedy film about a modern day Mexican officer who recaptures the Alamo. Although a reconstructed Alamo was built in Italy, the Daughters of the Republic of Texas, custodians of the Alamo, clashed with the film company during production in April 1969 when principal photography took place on Alamo Plaza (see Frank Thompson: *Alamo Movies*).

VOLLEY GUN

Seven-barrel flintlock muzzleloader invented by James Wilson in 1779 and created for the British Royal Navy in 1780 by Henry Nock. The so-called Nock Volley Gun, which fired all seven barrels simultaneously when the trigger was squeezed, was the primary weapon of Richard Widmark's Jim Bowie character in John Wayne's film *The Alamo* (see William Chemerka: "The Nock Volley Gun" in *The Alamo Journal*, #51, July 1986).

VON SCHMIDT, ERIC

Connecticut-based artist who created the enormous (23' long & 10' high) painting *The Storming of the Alamo* in 1986. The painting was showcased at San Antonio's Witte Museum during the Texas Sesquicentennial and featured in the March 1986 issue of *Smithsonian* magazine. The artist displayed several rarely-seen preliminary sketches of his work at the 1996 Alamo Society Symposium at Yale University's Beinecke Rare Book and Manuscript Library.

"WAGON TRAIN"

Popular western NBC-TV series which featured an Alamo-related episode, "The Jose Morales Story," on October 26, 1960. Morales (Lee Marvin) encounters an Alamo deserter named Rocque (Lon Chaney, Jr.), who redeems himself when he dies heroically during an Indian attack (see Frank Thompson: *Alamo Movies*).

WAGONEERS

Texas-based country band whose A&M Records debut LP in 1988, *Stout And High*, is a tribute to the walls of the Alamo (see "New Alamo 'Album'" in *The Alamo Journal*, #66, May 1989).

WALKER, ASA

Tennessee-born Alamo defender, 23, and cousin of artillerist Jacob Walker. Both Walkers were killed at the Alamo (see Walter Lord: *A Time To Stand*).

WALKER, JACOB

Tennessee-born artillerist, 37, and cousin of Alamo defender Asa Walker. Both Walkers were killed at the Alamo (see Walter Lord: *A Time To Stand*).

WARD, WILLIAM B.

Irish Alamo defender, 30, who was killed at the Alamo (see Daughters of the Republic of Texas: *The Alamo Long Barrack Museum*).

WARNELL, HENRY

Arkansas-born Alamo artillerist, 24, who was wounded at the Alamo and may have escaped. He probably died of his wounds several months later in Nacogdoches, Texas (see Walter Lord: *A Time To Stand*).

WASHINGTON, GEORGE

Alamo defender not currently acknowledged as one who participated in the thirteen-day siege and battle (see Thomas R. Lindley: "A Correct List of Alamo Patriots" in *The Alamo Journal*, #89, December 1993).

"*The Fugitive.*" *A sole Alamo defender (Henry Warnell?) survives the March 6, 1836 assault. Illustration by Gary Zaboly*

WASHINGTON, JOSEPH G.
Kentucky-born Alamo defender, 26, who was killed in the March 6 battle (see Daughters of the Republic of Texas: *The Alamo Long Barrack Museum*).

WATERS, MICHAEL
Founder of the Alamo Lore and Myth Organization and editor of its newsletter, *A.L.A.M.O.*, during its publication run from 1979 to 1982.

WATERS, THOMAS
English member of Captain Carey's artillery company, 24, who was killed at the Alamo (see Bill Groneman: *Alamo Defenders*).

WEAKLEY, MARK
Producer of the 1982 construction booklet, "Build the Alamo."

WEIGEL, CHARLES J., II
Author of 1948 pamphlet "The Alamo . . . Thermopylae of Texas."

WELLS, WILLIAM
Georgia-born Alamo defender, 37, who was killed in the March 6 battle (see Daughters of the Republic of Texas: *The Alamo Long Barrack Museum*).

"WHEN DAVY CROCKETT MET THE SAN ANTONIO ROSE"
Decca Records 45 rpm single written by Dave McEnery and performed by Red River Dave (McEnery). The single notes that the song was "recorded with the original authentic Davy Crockett fiddle, courtesy of the Witte Memorial Museum."

"WHERE LIE THE HEROES OF THE ALAMO? THE STORY OF A RARE DEVOTION"
Mrs. S. J. Wright's 1937 pamphlet about the Alamo defenders. The eighteen-page publication makes no specific mention of the death of David Crockett.

WHITE, ISAAC
Alamo defender of unknown age who came from either Arkansas or Kentucky. White was killed in the March 6 battle (see Bill Groneman: *Alamo Defenders*).

WHITE. ROBERT
Alamo defender who had commanded (as a captain) the Béxar Guards following the Battle of Béxar. White was killed at the Alamo (see Bill Groneman: *Alamo Defenders*).

WIDMARK, RICHARD
Veteran actor who played Jim Bowie in John Wayne's *The Alamo* (see Frank Thompson: *Alamo Movies*).

WILLIAMSON, HIRAM JAMES
Pennsylvania-born Alamo noncommissioned officer (sergeant major) who was killed in the March 6, 1836, battle (see Phil Rosenthal and Bill Groneman: *Roll Call at the Alamo*).

WILLS, WILLIAM
Alamo defender of unknown origin and birth who was killed in the March 6, 1836, battle (see Daughters of the Republic of Texas: *The Alamo Long Barrack Museum*).

WILSON, DAVID L.
Alamo defender, 29, who was born in Scotland. Wilson was killed in the March 6, 1836, battle (see Daughters of the Republic of Texas: *The Alamo Long Barrack Museum*).

WILSON, JOHN
Pennsylvania-born Alamo defender, 32, who was killed in the March 6, 1836, battle (see Daughters of the Republic of Texas: *The Alamo Long Barrack Museum*).

WINKLER, ERNEST WILLIAM
Author of 1916 pamphlet "The Alamo: A Memorial to Texan Heroism."

WLODARSKI, ROB AND ANNE
Husband and wife team who authored the 1996 book *The Haunted Alamo: A History of the Mission and Guide to Paranormal Activity*.

WOLF, ANTHONY
Alamo artillerist, 54, who had two sons with him, ages 11 and 12, during the thirteen-day siege. All three were killed in the March 6 battle, although the Wolf children were noncombatants (see Walter Lord: *A Time To Stand*).

WOLL, ADRIAN
Quartermaster (colonel) of Santa Anna's army in 1835-36 campaign. Six years later, as a general in 1842, Woll briefly occupied San Antonio (see Stephen L. Hardin: *Texian Iliad*).

WOOLSEY, WALLACE
Professor *emeritus* of foreign langauges at Texas Woman's University, who translated Gen. Vicente Filisola's *Memorias para la historia de la guerra de Tejas* (*Memoirs for the History of the War*) in Texas in 1985.

WOOLUMS, JAMES
Texas-based diorama builder who specializes in constructing the Alamo of both history and motion pictures. His firm, 1836 Replicas, was founded on March 6, 1993.

WRIGHT, CLAIRBORNE
North Carolina-born member of Gonzales Ranging Company, 26, who was killed in the March 6 battle (see Daughters of the Republic of Texas: *The Alamo Long Barrack Museum*).

WRIGHT, MRS. S. J.
Author of 1937 publication, *Our Living Alamo* and *Where Lie the Heroes of the Alamo?: The Story of a Rare Devotion*.

VAUGHAN, ROBERT
Author of the 1996 fictional novel *Texas Glory: An Epic of the Alamo*.

YELVINGTON, RAMSEY
Playwright who penned 1960 production *The Drama of the Alamo*.

YENA, DONALD M.
Painter of *The Alamo — March 6, 1836*, a 1967 oil whose point of view is from the attacking Mexicans outside the compound's northwest corner (see Susan Prendergast Schoelwer: *Alamo Images: Changing Perceptions of a Texas Experience*).

YOHN, FREDERICK C.
Illustrator of *The Battle of the Alamo*, a 1913 print which focuses on Crockett's final moments in front of the Alamo

chapel (see Susan Prendergast Schoelwer: *Alamo Images: Changing Perceptions of a Texas Experience*).

YORK, JOHN
Texian infantry captain in Ben Milam's First Division during Siege and Battle of Béxar in 1835 (Alwyn Barr: *Texans in Revolt*).

"YOU ARE THERE"
History-based CBS-TV series (1953-57) that aired "The Defense of the Alamo" on May 24, 1953. The series was revived briefly in 1971-72 and broadcast a "Siege of the Alamo" episode on October 9, 1971, which starred Fred Gwynne as David Crockett (see Frank Thompson: *Alamo Movies*).

YOUNG, KEVIN
Historical/technical consultant who contributed to a number of Alamo books, films, and TV projects including *Alamo . . . The Price of Freedom* and *James Michener's "Texas."* Young was the keynote speaker at the first meeting of the Alamo Defenders Descendants Association on March 5, 1995.

"YOUNG RIDERS"
Western ABC-TV series which aired an Alamo-related episode, "Then There Was One," in 1990 about a crazed Alamo courier who is murdering the other surviving messengers twenty-five years after the famous siege (see Mike Boldt: "The Young Riders: An 'Alamo' Episode" in *The Alamo Journal*, #71, June 1990).

ZABOLY, GARY
New York-based artist who painted *Travis' Line* (1990). Zaboly also created a number of pen and ink drawings for Stephen L. Hardin's *Texian Iliad* and such historical publications as the *Military Collector & Historian* and *The Alamo Journal*, among others.

ZAMBRANO, JUAN A.
Goliad-area Tejano who served as a spy for Stephen Austin in Matamoros but was captured by Juan Jose Urrea's forces (see Paul Lack: *The Texas Revolutionary Experience*).

ZAMBRANO ROW

Group of buildings in San Antonio de Béxar that was the scene of fighting between Mexican forces under General Cos and Texians under Col. Frank Johnson following the death of Ben Milam on December 7, 1835. The Mexicans eventually abandoned Zambrano Row (see Stephen L. Hardin: *Texian Iliad*).

ZANCO, CHARLES

Danish Alamo officer (lieutenant in Ordnance Department), 28, (real name: Charles Lanco) who may have created the first "lone star" flag in late 1835. He was killed in the March 6, 1836, battle (see Thomas R. Lindley: "A Correct List of Alamo Patriots" in *The Alamo Journal*, #89, December 1993).

ZAPADORES BATTALION

Highly-regarded Mexican infantry unit in Col. Antonio Gaona's First Brigade which was organized into a reserve group with other units under Col. Augustin Amat in the March 6, 1836, Alamo assault (see Albert Nofi: *The Alamo and the Texas War for Independence*).

ZUBER, WILLIAM P.

Individual who suggested in "An Escape from the Alamo," an article in the 1873 edition of the *Texas Almanac*, that Travis drew a line with sword and asked the members of the Alamo garrison to cross it if they were willing to remain and fight. According to Zuber, the story of Travis' dramatic action was told to him by Moses Rose, who allegedly escaped from the Alamo during the siege. The Zuber account, which lacks documentation and is highly suspect, is the sole source of the Travis line-drawing episode. Zuber also wrote an eleven-page manuscript, *The Funeral in the Alamo*, which is currently stored in the Texas State Archives.

ZUCKER, DAVID

California-based motion picture director-producer-writer and Davy Crockett memorabilia collector who included several Alamo and Crockett embellishments in his three *Naked Gun* comedy films. Zucker even briefly appeared as a buckskin-clad, flintlock-shooting Crockett in *Naked Gun 2 1/2*. Zucker first made public his plans for a major film on Crockett in 1991 (see William Chemerka: "Zucker's Next Film: Davy Crockett?" in *The Alamo Journal*, #79, December 1991).

ZZ TOP

Texas-based hard rock 'n' blues trio (Billy Gibbons, guitar; Dusty Hill, bass; and Frank Beard, drums) which recorded a 1979 album titled *Deguello* (Warner Bros. Records) after the famous Mexican bugle call which signaled the March 6, 1836, attack on the Alamo. Noted Gibbons in an 1980 interview: "It's kind of a shame how (the Alamo) looks today. But it's got its history" (see William Chemerka: "ZZ Top: That Little Ol' Band From The Lone Star State Shoots For Outer Space" in *The Aquarian Weekly*, #329, August 27, 1980).

Louis Eyth. The Speech of Travis to His Men at the Alamo.
From a copyprint in the Daughters of the Republic of Texas Library at the Alamo.

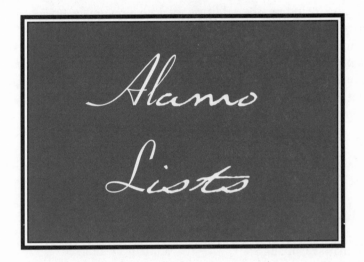

Alamo
Lists

BIRTHPLACES OF THE 189
ALAMO DEFENDERS

This roster includes the most recent research on birthplaces, including the addition of two previously unacknowledged states: Maine and New Hampshire. According to researcher Edward Dubravsky of Maine, John Flanders and William Linn, two defenders traditionally identified as being from Massachusetts were actually born in other New England states ("Alamo Defender From New Hampshire" in *The Alamo Journal*, #95, February 1995, and "William Linn — Alamo Defender" in *The Alamo Journal*, #101, June 1996).

Also, some of the following names were probably not Alamo defenders. See "Alamo Roll Call Changes According To Texian Army Investigations" list.

ALABAMA (4)
James Buchanan
William Fishbaugh
Galba Fuqua
William D. Sutherland

ARKANSAS (3)
Isaac G. Baker
Jesse G. Thompson
Henry Warnell

CONNECTICUT (1)
Gordon C. Jennings

DENMARK (1)
Charles Zanco

ENGLAND (12)
William Blazeby
Daniel Bourne
George Brown
Stephen Dennison

James R. Dimpkins
James C. Gwynne
William D. Hersee
Marcus L. Sewell
Richard Starr
James E. Stewart
Thomas Waters
Anthony Wolf

GEORGIA (5)
Albert C. Grimes
Eliel Melton
Edward T. Mitchell
Mansom Shied
William Wells

GERMANY (2)
Henry Courtman
Henry Thomas

ILLINOIS (1)
Jonathan L. Lindley

IRELAND (12)

Samuel E. Burns
Andrew Duvalt
Robert Evans
Joseph M. Hawkins
William D. Jackson
Thomas Jackson
James McGee
Robert McKinney
James Nowlan
Jackson J. Rusk
Burke Trammel
William B. Ward

KENTUCKY (13)

Peter James Bailey
James Bowie
Daniel W. Cloud
Jacob Darst
John Davis
William H. Furtleroy
John E. Gaston
John Harris
Green B. Jameson
Andrew Kent
Joseph Rutherford
B. A. M. Thomas
Isaac White

LOUISIANA (4)

Charles Despallier
James W. Garrand
Joseph Kerr
Isaac Ryan

MAINE (1)

William Linn

MARYLAND (1)

Charles S. Smith

MASSACHUSETTS (3)

Robert Crossman
William D. Howell
Amos Pollard

MISSISSIPPI (4)

Isaac Millsaps
Willis Moore
George Pagan
Christopher Parker

MISSOURI (5)

William C. Baker
George D. Butler
Charles H. Clark
Jerry C. Day
George W. Tumlinson

NEW HAMPSHIRE (1)

John Flanders

NEW JERSEY (1)

Robert E. Cochran

NEW YORK (7)

Robert Cunningham
Lewis Duel
Samuel B. Evans
John H. Forsyth
John Jones
George Kimball
James Tylee

NORTH CAROLINA (7)

Micajah Autry
Dolphin W. Floyd
William Parks
Mial Scurlock
Joshua G. Smith
John W. Thompson
Claiborne Wright

OHIO (3)
William B. Harrison
Tapley Holland
Robert Musselman

PENNSYLVANIA (10)
James Brown
John Cane
David Cummings
Samuel Holloway
William Johnson
William McDowell
John P. Reynolds
John M. Thurston
Hiram J. Williamson
John Wilson

RHODE ISLAND (1)
Albert Martin

SCOTLAND (4)
Robert W. Ballentine
John McGregor
Isaac Robertson
David L. Wilson

SOUTH CAROLINA (7)
James B. Bonham
Lemuel Crawford
George Neggan
Edward Nelson
George Nelson
Cleveland K. Simmons
William B. Travis

TEJAS (9)
Juan Abamillo
Juan Badillo
Carlos Espalier
Gregorio Esparza
Antonio Fuentes

Jose M. Guerrero
Damacio Jimenez
Toribio D. Losoya
Andres Nava

TENNESSEE (31)
Joseph Bayliss
John Blair
Samuel C. Blair
Robert Campbell
George W. Cottle
David Crockett
Squire Daymon
William Dearduff
Almeron Dickinson
John H. Dillard
James L. Ewing
William Garnett
James G. Garrett
John C. Goodrich
Charles M. Haskell (Heiskell)
John M. Hays
William Marshall
Jesse McCoy
Thomas R. Miller
William Mills
Andrew M. Nelson
James Robertson
Andrew H. Smith
A. Spain Summerlin
William E. Summers
Edward Taylor
George Taylor
William Taylor
Asa Walker
Jacob Walker
Joseph G. Washington

VERMONT (1)
Miles D. Andross

VIRGINIA (14)
Robert Allen
John J. Baugh
William R. Carey
Patrick H. Herndon
James Kenney
William I. Lewis
William J. Lightfoot
George W. Main
William T. Malone
Edward F. Mitchusson
Robert B. Moore
James Northcross
James M. Rose
Richard L. Stockton

WALES (1)
Lewis Johnson

UNKNOWN (19)
John J. Ballentine

Jesse B. Bowman
Robert Brown
M. B. Clark
Freeman H. K. Day
John E. Garvin
James George
James Hannum
Andrew J. Harrison
Johnnie Kellogg
William P. King
Edward McCafferty
Napoleon B. Mitchell
Richardson Perry
Thomas H. Roberts
William H. Smith
Robert White
William Wills
"John"

ALAMO ROLL CALL CHANGES ACCORDING TO TEXIAN ARMY INVESTIGATIONS

Texian Army Investigations is an Austin, Texas-based history research enterprise created by Thomas Ricks Lindley. According to Lindley, not only should names be added to the Alamo's roll call of heroes, but some names currently listed should be deleted.

NAMES THAT SHOULD BE ADDED

1. I. L. K. Harrison
2. Conrad Eigenauer
3. A. Anderson
4. James Holloway
5. T. P. Hutchinson
6. John Morman

7. William Spratt
8. George Washington
9. William George
10. Jacob Roth

NAMES THAT COULD BE ADDED

1. John Kelley
2. Francis H. Gray
3. William Harrel
4. J. H. Sanders
5. Alexander E. Patton
6. James R. Munson
7. Moses Buttler
8. Phillip Roaches
9. B. F. Shaw
10. Charles C. Haskiel
11. H. H. Kirk

NAMES THAT SHOULD BE DELETED

1. John Kellogg
2. Jose Maria Guerrero
3. Isaac Robinson
4. Jerry Day
5. Jesse B. Bowman
6. Jesse G. Thompson

ALAMO SURVIVORS

A number of noncombatants, primarily Tejano women and children, survived the March 6, 1836, battle. Susanna Dickinson and her fifteen-month-old daughter were the only Anglo noncombatants. Joe was William B. Travis' slave. There is a possibility that several other slaves, including "Bettie" and "Charlie," were inside the Alamo. Thomas Ricks Lindley of Texian Army Investigations of Austin, Texas, suggests that Brigido Guerrero (an alleged combatant who survived the battle by convincing the Mexican soldiers that he had been captured by the Texians) may not have been at the Alamo at all.

Alsbury, Juana Navarro
"Bettie"
"Charlie"
De Salinas, Victoriana and three small daughters
Dickinson, Angelina
Dickinson, Susanna
Esparza, Ana (Salazar)
Esparza, Enrique (son of Ana Esparza and José Gregorio Esparza)
Esparza, Francisco (son of Ana Esparza and José Gregorio Esparza)
Esparza, Manuel (son of Ana Esparza and José Gregorio Esparza)
Esparza, Maria de Jesus Castro (daughter of Ana Esparza and Victor de Castro)
Gonzales, Petra
Guerrero, Brigido
"Joe" (a slave belonging to William B. Travis)
Losoya, Concepcion
Losoya, Juan
Melton, Juana Francisca Losoya
Navarro, Gertrudis (sister of Juana Navarro Alsbury)
Perez Jr., Alijo (son of Juana N. Alsbury and Alijo Perez)
Saucedo, Trinidad (according to Enrique Esparza, Saucedo left during an armistice)

ALAMO OFFICERS WHO DIED AT THE BATTLE OF THE ALAMO

Baker, William C. M.	Captain
Baugh, John J.	Captain
Blair, Samuel C.	Captain
Blazeby, William	Captain
Bonham, James B.	Lieutenant
Bowie, James	Colonel
Campbell, Robert	Lieutenant
Carey, William R.	Captain
Dickinson, Almeron	Captain
Forsyth, John H.	Captain
Harrison, William B.	Captain
Jameson, Green	Major
Jones, John	Lieutenant
Kimball, George C.	Lieutenant
McCafferty, Edward	Lieutenant
Martin, Albert	Captain
Melton, Eliel	Lieutenant
Simmons, Cleveland K.	Lieutenant
Travis, William B.	Lt. Colonel (commander)
Thruston, John M.	Second Lieutenant
White, Robert	Captain
Zanco, Charles	Lieutenant

Master of Ordnance Robert Evans may have held the rank of major.

Noncommissioned officers included:
Sgt. Juan A. Badillo, Sgt. William Hersee, Sgt. Robert Musselman, Sgt. William B. Ward, Sgt. Maj. Hiram J. Williamson, and Third Corporal William J. Lightfoot. David Crockett served as a private.

ALAMO COURIERS

This traditional roster identifies those who left the Alamo and sought help for the threatened garrison. Recent research, however, suggests that some of these couriers (Antonio Cruz y Arocha, John W. Baylor, Robert Brown, Byrd Lockhart, William S. Oury, Andrew Sowell and John Sutherland) may not have been inside the Alamo during the siege. Those couriers identified with an asterisk (*) were killed during the March 6 assault.

Allen, James L.
Arocha, Antonio Cruz y
Baylor, John W.
Bonham, James B. *
Brown, Robert *
Despallier, Charles *
Highsmith, Benjamin F.
Lockhart, Byrd

Martin, Albert *
Oury, William S.
Seguin, Juan N.
Smith, John W.
Smithers, Lancelot
Sowell, Andrew J.
Sutherland, John

THE GONZALES 32

This traditional roster of men (actually the Gonzales Ranging Company) who came to the defense of the Alamo on March 1, 1836, may not be correct. Thomas Ricks Lindley of Texian Army Investigations in Austin, Texas, suggests that John Kellogg, for example, died in Harrisburg, Texas, during the autumn of 1836. Also, John W. Smith is known to have left the Alamo on March 3 as a courier.

Baker, Isaac G.
Cane, John
Cottle, George W.
Cummings, David P.
Darst, Jacob C.
Davis, John
Daymon, Squire

Dearduff, William
Despallier, Charles
Fishbaugh, William
Flanders, John
Floyd, Dolphin W.
Fuqua, Galba
Garvin, John E.

Gaston, John E.
George, James
Martin, Albert
Jackson, Thomas
Kellogg, John
Kent, Andrew
Kimball, George C.
King, William P.
Lindley, Jonathan L.

McCoy, Jesse
Miller, Thomas R.
Millsaps, Isaac
Neggan, George
Smith, John W.
Summers, William E.
Tumlinson, George W.
White, Robert
Wright, Claiborne

ALAMO NUMBERS

1   # of dollars per month paid by the United States Army to the City of San Antonio to lease the Alamo as a quartermaster depot (contract filed on June 10, 1853).

2   # of movies with Alamo in the title that have nothing to do with the 1836 Battle of the Alamo (*Last Stand at the Alamo* and *Alamo Bay*).

3   # of Mexican assault columns on March 6, 1836, with over three hundred men.

4   # of identified defenders on the Alamo Cenotaph (Crockett, Bowie, Travis, and Bonham).

5   # of Alamo defenders executed following the battle in *Houston: The Legend of Texas*.

6   # of times the word "Alamo" is used in John Wayne's *The Alamo*.

7   # of movies filmed at Happy Shahan's Alamo Village that feature the Alamo.

8   # of days into the Alamo siege when the Gonzales Ranging Company arrived.

9   # of Alamo movies made since the Texas Centennial.

10	# of teenage Alamo defenders.
11	# of Tejano females who survived the Battle of the Alamo.
12	# of Alamo defenders who were older than forty.
13	# of days in the siege of the Alamo.
14	# of modern properties needed to be purchased in order to restore the Alamo to its 1836 appearance.
21	# of artillery pieces in the Alamo during the siege.
31	# of Alamo defenders who were born in Tennessee.
39	# of Spaniards allegedly buried on the Alamo grounds, according to Gary Gabehart, president of the Inter-Tribal Council of American Indians.
46	% of Alamo visitors in the 1990s who believe twentieth century-built Alamo garden walls existed in 1836, according to the *San Antonio Express-News*.
165	# of feet (height) in never-built early twentieth century Alamo monument proposed by Alamo Monument Association.
168	# of people (out of 394) who rated John Wayne's *The Alamo* "great" following a preview of the film at the Aladdin Theatre in Denver, Colorado, on August 5, 1960. Another 179 people rated the film "excellent."
189	# of Alamo defenders currently acknowledged at the Alamo as having died there in the March 6, 1836, battle.
192	# of minutes running time of John Wayne's *The Alamo* before it was edited down to 161 minutes.
257	# of Alamo defenders who probably died at the March 6, 1836, battle.
586	# of commercial listings that begin with the word

"Alamo" in the white pages of the San Antonio, Texas, telephone directory.

802   # of feet (height) in never-built Alamo monument column designed by architect Alfred Giles in 1912.

921   # of Native Americans allegedly buried on Alamo grounds, according to Gary Gabehart, president of the Inter-Tribal Council of American Indians.

3,000,000   # of people (approximately) who visit the Alamo each year.

8,000,000   # of dollars that John Wayne's *The Alamo* grossed during its initial run.

12,000,000   # of dollars that John Wayne's *The Alamo* cost to make.

32,616,900   # of dollars needed to purchase adjacent property around the Alamo and restore the garrison to its 1836 appearance according to a 1994 estimate by the *San Antonio Express-News*.

ROSTER OF PRESIDENTS GENERAL OF THE DAUGHTERS OF THE REPUBLIC OF TEXAS*

President general is the highest elected office within the ranks of the Daughters of the Republic of Texas, the state-appointed custodians of the Alamo.

Mrs. Anson Jones	1891-1908
Mrs. Rebecca Jane Fisher	1908-1927
Mrs. Clara Driscoll	1927-1931
Mrs. O. M. Farnsworth	1931-1935
Mrs. Carrie Franklin Kemp (acting president)	1935-1937
Mrs. Frederick Schenkenberg	1939-1941
Mrs. Ben F. Edwards	1941-1943
Mrs. Walter Prescott Webb	1943-1945
Mrs. Paul Lobit	1945-1947
Mrs. Henry R. Maresh	1947-1949
Mrs. Henry R. Wofford, Sr.	1949-1951
Mrs. H. C. Vandervoort	1951-1953
Mrs. Edna Hinde	1953-1955
Mrs. Barclay Megarity	1955-1957
Mrs. Joe N. Sanderson	1957-1959
Mrs. H. Raymond Hagan	1959-1961
Mrs. Murray Ezell	1961-1963
Miss Sarah Milita Hill	1963-1965
Mrs. Robert F. Hallock	1965-1967
Mrs. William Lawrence Scarborough	1967-1969
Miss Naomi-Ray Morey	1969-1971
Mrs. M. M. O'Dowd	1971-1973
Mrs. George Plunkett Red	1973-1975
Mrs. Hugh B. Lowery	1975-1977
Mrs. Eugene M. Addison	1977-1979
Mrs. George F. Hollis	1979-1981
Mrs. B. F. McKinney	1981-1983
Mrs. Rex L. Arnold	1983-1985

Mrs. Grady D. Rash, Jr.	1985-1987
Mrs. Henry L. Averitee	1987-1989
Mrs. Donald Oscar Naylor	1989-1991
Mrs. Betty Fagan Burr	1991-1993
Mrs. Gail Loving Barnes	1993-1995
Mrs. Mary Kathryn Spiller Briggs	1995-

* An exclusive entry for *The Alamo Almanac & Book of Lists.*

TOP 20 MOST FREQUENTLY ASKED
QUESTIONS AT THE ALAMO*
(Directed at the Alamo's Historical Interpreters)

1. "Where's the bathroom?"
2. "Is this the real Alamo?"
3. "Has the Alamo been moved?"
4. "Did Daniel Boone die here?"
5. "Where's the IMAX Theatre?"
6. "Is this the original or is it manmade?"
7. "Where did Davy Crockett die?"
8. "Is this a national park?"
9. "Where are the Alamo defenders buried?"
10. "How much does it cost to get in?"
11. "Where's the basement?"
12. "Are these marks in the walls bullet holes?"
13. "What happened here?"
14. "Where did Travis die?"
15. "Where did Bowie die?"
16. "When was the roof and floor added?"
17. "How many Alamo defenders died here?"
18. "How many Mexican soldiers died here?"
19. "Why didn't anyone come to the aid of the Alamo?"
20. "What makes the Alamo defenders heroes?"

* An exclusive entry for *The Alamo Almanac & Book of Lists.*

ALAMO CURATORS*

The office of curator of the Alamo is only thirty years old, although members of the Daughters of the Republic of Texas have served as "custodians" of the Shrine of Texas Liberty for nearly a century.

1966-1967   Samuel Nesmith
1968   James K. Nutt
1970-1985   Charles Long (*Curator Emeritus*)
1985-1990   Steve Beck
1990   Pierce Grisham (acting Curator)
1990-1995   Wallay Saage
1996-   Dr. Richard Bruce Winders

("Any listing of curators at the Alamo should begin with the efforts of Sarah Elizabeth Eager, Mrs. Fannie Applewhite and Mrs. Lieta Small. Their correspondence is signed 'custodian.' They would have been in a position of educating visitors to the Alamo of its history and in some cases receiving donations to the Alamo Collections. Most certainly supervision and exhibit of those items were their responsibilities," noted former curator Saage in 1995.)

* An exclusive entry for *The Alamo Almanac & Book of Lists.*

CHARLES J. LONG'S MOST INTERESTING
UNANSWERED ALAMO QUESTIONS *

Charles J. Long, a native of Newark, New Jersey, was the curator at the Alamo from 1970 to 1985. He served longer in that position than anyone else. During his tenure at the Shrine of Texas Liberty, Long assisted numerous researchers, writers, and historians. Even after he retired, he still provided assistance on a number of Alamo projects. In 1986, for example, he helped design and supervise the construction and installation of the Alamo church's replacement doors after a fire had damaged the previous ones. Long can still be found at the Daughters of the Republic of Texas Library at the Alamo every Friday. For Long, a number of Alamo questions remain unanswered, but these have intrigued him for years.

1) The Esparza Account
Was the 1907 newspaper account of the Siege and Battle of the Alamo recollected by noncombatant Enrique Esparza and printed in The *San Antonio Daily Express* on May 12 and May 19, 1907, truthful? "An eyewitness account seventy years later? An amazing memory! Yet, he is quoted by many writers and historians. I have found no back-up versions to help his stories."

2) The Lightfoot Survival
Was Virginia-born William J. Lightfoot actually an Alamo survivor? "A Lightfoot descendant claimed he survived, lived in East Texas, and was killed by a bunch of night riders. The descendant is one of the millions of people who insist they are going to write a book about their ancestor. However, these books usually never get published, and the story or historical information disappears."

3) The Fate of the Wolf Family
Were Anthony Wolf's two children with him during the Siege and Battle of the Alamo? And were these two unarmed youngsters, ages 11 and 12, killed on March 6 by Santa Anna's

soldiers? "The Wolf story has been muddied by many people starting with our Esparza 'eyewitness.' According to records, Wolf was married to a widow in Natchitoches, Louisiana. They had one son who lived and died in Texas. I am waiting for the next version."

4) The Cochran Genealogy

Where exactly did New Jersey-born Alamo defender Robert Cochran come from? He died during the March 6, 1836, battle, and Cochran County, Texas, is named in his honor. "He was either born or lived in Kearny, New Jersey. He traveled to Boston, boarded a boat and sailed to New Orleans. He probably joined the New Orleans Greys. This group traveled to San Antonio for the Battle of Béxar. Some Grays left; Cochran stayed and got killed three months later in the Battle of the Alamo."

5) The Bowie Family

James Bowie's wife and two children allegedly died as a result of cholera in Mexico in 1833. "Did James Bowie have two children? There are no birth or baptismal records. One clerk at the Béxar County Courthouse named the two children. The Mormon records list the two children. Their source is this same anonymous clerk at the courthouse who left years ago. Where she found this information cannot be located. The Monclova, Mexico, death records from the cholera epidemic mention Bowie's wife, her father and servants, but no children. Bowie prepared his will at this time without knowledge of the events in Monclova. He mentions his wife but does not mention any children."

* An exclusive entry for *The Alamo Almanac & Book of Lists*.

15 HISTORICAL DESCRIPTIONS
OF THE ALAMO

1. "A symbol of valor."
   John Myers Myers, author, *The Alamo*, 1948

2. "A mere wreck of its former grandeur."
   Frederick Law Olmstead, writer, 1854

3. "Kind of a shame."
   Billy Gibbons, guitarist, rock trio ZZ Top, 1980

4. "A broken down fort."
   John Wayne as Davy Crockett in *The Alamo*, 1960

5. "Unimpressive."
   Weissmann Reports, tourist information organization, 1995

6. "A fortress all in ruins that the weeds have overgrown."
   Marty Robbins, singer, "Ballad of the Alamo," 1960

7. "Shrine of Texas Liberty."
   San Antonio Express, 1905

8. "The facade of Texas history."
   Michael Grant, author, *Deep in the Heart of Texas*, 1991

9. "The most-visited historical site in Texas."
   Paseo del Rio Showboat promotional magazine, 1981

10. "A symbol of the problem in our relationship with Mexico."
    Arizona Governor Bruce Babbitt, 1979

11. "A Hispanic building dedicated to Anglo-Texan glories."
    Susan Prendergast Schoelwer in *Alamo Images: Changing Perceptions of a Texas Experience,* 1985

12. "The key of Texas."
    William B. Travis, 1836

13. "Hallowed ground."
    Virginia May Moffitt, author, *Remember the Alamo!*, 1953

14. "A great attraction, one time."
    Rick Casey in the *San Antonio Monthly*, 1986

15. "A treasured American symbol."
    Fess Parker in *Alamo Movies,* 1991

BEST ALAMO BOOKS *

In 1991 members of the Alamo Society cast votes for their favorite Alamo books of all time. Walter Lord, who penned the organization's favorite volume, *A Time To Stand*, was presented with an award plaque at the Alamo Restaurant in New York City on March 6, 1991. The presentation coincided with the book's thirtieth anniversary of being in print.

TOP THREE

#1 *A Time To Stand* by Walter Lord, 1961

#2 *Alamo Images: Changing Perceptions of a Texas Experience* by Susan Prendergast Schoelwer (introduction by Dr. Paul Hutton), 1985

#3 *13 Days to Glory* by Lon Tinkle, 1958

Honorable Mentions:

Exploring the Alamo Legends by Wallace Chariton, 1990

The Alamo by John Myers Myers, 1948

Alamo Movies by Frank Thompson, 1991

Roll Call at the Alamo by Phil Rosenthal and Bill Groneman, 1985

Alamo . . . The Price of Freedom by George McAlister, 1988

Remember the Alamo by Robert Penn Warren, 1958

Alamo Defenders by Bill Groneman, 1990

100 Days in Texas: The Alamo Letters by Wallace Chariton, 1990

Best New Alamo Book Since the 1991 Poll:

Texian Iliad by Stephen L. Hardin, 1994

* An exclusive entry for *The Alamo Almanac & Book of Lists*.

TOP 10 MODERN "REMEMBER THE ALAMO" BUSINESSES

In 1836 the Alamo represented bravery, sacrifice, and courage. Today the Alamo's name represents other qualities as well. Here are some unique San Antonio area-based Alamo businesses to remember!

Alamo Air Duct & Carpet Cleaning
Alamo Area Square and Round Dance Association
Alamo Balloons
Alamo Barber & Beauty Supply
Alamo Chimney Sweep
Alamo City Pest Control
Alamo Dog & Cat Grooming
Alamo Sewer Service
Alamo Volleyball
Alamo Wigs

(Source: Southwestern Bell Telephone Company White Pages, Greater San Antonio, 1995.)

TOP 10 UTILITARIAN ALAMO GIFTS

The Alamo church has been recreated in a number of useful, three-dimensional ways over the years. Here are ten to remember — and purchase!

Alamo Bank   Alamo Magnet
Alamo Bird House   Alamo Mailbox
Alamo Book Ends   Alamo Paper Weights
Alamo Candle Holders   Alamo Pencil Sharpener
Alamo Key Chains   Alamo Salt & Pepper Shakers

TEXAS BOB'S LIST
OF THE TACKIEST (BUT ENJOYABLE)
ALAMO COLLECTIBLES*

Texas Bob Reinhardt's Art Showcase of pop culture collectibles has been featured in such publications as the *Wall
Street Journal, TV Guide, Texas Monthly,* and *Playboy,* among
others. Among his diverse Alamo collectibles are these kitchy,
offbeat offerings.

1. Alamo Natural Charcoal
This five-pound-bag (produced by the Alamo Fuel Company
in San Antonio), which features a drawing of the chapel on
the front, contains these words: "Recommended for people
who enjoy and understand the natural flavor that goes in good
meat." Regardless of the recommendation, this is undoubted-
ly the most "tasteless" comment, considering that the Alamo
defenders were burned to ashes!

2. Alamo Fruitcake Tin
This deluxe fruitcake tin made by the Collin Street Bakery in
Corsicana, Texas, features a Currier & Ives-type Christmas
scene on its lid, complete with a cowboy twirling a lariat in
front of a star with the Alamo in the background!

3. Alamo Booze
W. L. Weller bourbon in a commemorative Texas sesquicentennial decanter, complete with a small reproduction of Onderdonk's *Fall of the Alamo* painting. But the painting, which
depicts dramatic fighting in the Alamo courtyard between the
chapel and South Wall, is practically covered up by the sesquicentennial flag logo! However, portraits of Travis, Bowie,
Crockett, and Bonham are on either side of the label.

4. Texas Seasons Ice Cream
"White Christmas" half-gallon container features white
chocolate almond chunks in French vanilla ice cream. The
container, made by H.E.B food stores in San Antonio, has a

drawing of the Alamo in a snow globe paperweight on top of holly!

5. Alamo Coffee
Texas Hero Company "Alamo blend" gourmet coffee distributed by Design It in Huntsville, Texas. The company even makes a brand called "Crockett's Chocolate Raspberry!"

* An exclusive entry for *The Alamo Almanac & Book of Lists.*

MURRAY WEISSMANN'S 10 RAREST ALAMO COLLECTIBLES*

Dr. Murray Weissmann is a New Jersey radiologist who owns the world's largest private collection of Alamo and Davy Crockett memorabilia. Part of his collection is featured in the 1996 book *The Davy Crockett Craze.* He lists some of the most interesting (and valuable!) Alamo items in his vast collection.

1. "The Alamo" Holster Set. Produced by New York's McKinnon Leather Products, this two-gun holster set is the only known toy produced in conjunction with the release of John Wayne's film, *The Alamo,* in 1960. The original box depicts Wayne as Crockett about to draw his six-shooter!

2. Wedgwood Centennial Plate. A nine-inch blue and white Texas Centennial plate with scalloped borders, sponsored by the Mary Isham Keith Chapter, D.A.R., Fort Worth, Texas. The Alamo is depicted in the center, bordered by images of Austin, Houston, and the surrender scene of Santa Anna at San Jacinto.

3. "The Alamo" Premiere Tickets. A pair of unused tickets for the world premiere of John Wayne's film. The tickets, dated October 24, 1960, were for an 8:15 P.M. performance at the Woodlawn Theatre in San Antonio. These tickets remain in the original printed envelope, which is marked "Alamo World Premiere Committee of the San Antonio Chamber of Commerce."

4. "Davy Crockett at the Alamo" Art. Original galley sheet used to produce page 7 of Walt Disney's "Davy Crockett at the Alamo" comic book (Dell #639) published in 1955. The sheet is labeled D.C.O.S. #639 p. 7 and depicts Crockett's meeting with Thimblerig on the riverboat.

5. "Border Battle" Playset. Miniature (H.O. scale) playset, produced by Louis Marx and Company and made in Hong Kong. Manufactured at the time of John Wayne's film, "Border Battle" is essentially a reissue of the company's "Walt Disney Official Davy Crockett at the Alamo" playset from a few years earlier. Unlike the larger playsets, all the plastic buildings, accessories, and figures are hand painted.

6. Centennial Plaster Bank. Produced for the Texas Centennial in 1936, this Alamo-shaped bank features a slot at the top of the chapel's distinctive hump.

7. Alamo Bagatelle Game. A metal bagatelle game (made by Joseph Schneider, Inc. of New York) with graphics that depict the Battle of the Alamo, played with marbles like a table-top pinball game. Each Alamo defender and each sombrero and serape-wearing Mexican soldier is pictured next to a hole that corresponds to a specific point value.

8. Davy Crockett's Almanac. Original copy of Vol. 1, No. 3., published in Nashville, Tennessee in 1837 with graphics of "Fall of the Alamo . . . Death of Crockett." The image depicts Crockett being killed during the battle.

9. John Wayne Alamo Mug. One of the ceramic coffee mugs given to members of the cast and crew of *The Alamo* by John Wayne. The mug features a gold-painted handle and a picture of the battle-scarred Alamo chapel. Inscribed to "Ray from Duke."

10. "Remember the Alamo! Jigsaw Puzzle. Produced by Landmark Books to coincide with the release of the Random House book of the same name. The 20" x 14" 500-piece puzzle (in the original box) reproduces the book's Alamo battle scene cover art.

* An exclusive entry for *The Alamo Almanac & Book of Lists.*

FRANK THOMPSON'S FIVE BEST
ALAMO MOVIES*

Frank Thompson is a writer and film historian. His books include *Alamo Movies; Texas' First Picture Show; William A. Wellman; Lost Movies;* and *Robert Wise: A Bio-Bibliography,* among others. He has written several scripts and hundreds of articles, interviews, and reviews.

1. *The Alamo* (1960)
Big, colorful and genuinely moving, John Wayne's passionate hymn to patriotic sacrifice is not even close to great cinema — but it sure takes roots in the viewers' hearts and minds. And it co-stars Linda Cristal. *Ooh la la.*

2. *Davy Crockett, King of the Wild Frontier* (1955)
Ostensibly a child's version of Crockett's life, Davy Crockett is the only Alamo movie that conveys a sense of siege. Nearly all of the characters are fictional, yet their deaths are the most tragic and poignant in any Alamo film.

3. *Man of Conquest* (1939)
Republic's sprawling biography of Sam Houston has only a brief Alamo sequence but it has such an aura of authenticity that few Alamo movies can match. For once, the defenders aren't fur-clad mountain men itching for a rough-and-tumble fight, but average citizens of 1836, pushed to the point of revolution.

4. *Alamo . . . The Price of Freedom* (1988)
For once, the costuming and weaponry are fairly authentic, and the final battle of March 6, 1836, is fought, properly, in the dark. The magnificent IMAX imagery and the emotion of the closing montage almost make up for the worst acting in any Alamo movie.

5. *Heroes of the Alamo* (1937)
Did someone say bad acting? This cheater production has plenty, not to mention incredibly chintzy production values.

But its focus on Almeron and Susannah Dickinson is refreshing and there are genuinely interesting ideas and authentic historical points in the script. A bad movie, but a fascinating one.

Honorable mention: *The Last Command* (1955) Better than some.

* An exclusive entry for *The Alamo Almanac & Book of Lists.*

FRANK THOMPSON'S FIVE WORST ALAMO MOVIES*

1. *James A. Michener's "Texas"* (1994)
An unspeakably awful Frankenstein monster, created in part from the rotting corpses of several better Alamo movies. Execrable acting, scripting, costuming. The Fall of the Alamo is depicted entirely through a bad color print of *The Last Command* (1955) and the slow motion Battle of San Jacinto is like watching paint dry, except less interesting. The only positive thing to say about *Texas* is that it contains the most pointless and gratuitous nude scenes of any film in memory. Hey, it's something.

2. *The Time Tunnel: "The Alamo"* (1966)
Okay it's not exactly an Alamo movie, but it is one of the worst depictions of the Alamo on film. Our two bad-luck time travelers land at the Alamo on March 6 only to learn two depressing facts: Davy Crockett "died yesterday" (!) and the final assault is planned for five that afternoon (!). The Dickinsons, for reasons best known to the "writers," are here called Reynerson. This is television at its most insufferably stupid. Well, it was until *James A. Michener's "Texas"* came along.

3. *The Alamo* (1960)
Those of us who love it, do so in spite of its faults — which are legion. The script is banal, inaccurate, preachy and cliched, the acting is usually careless, the characters (with few excep-

tions) are two-dimensional and the humor forced and inappropriate. So why have I watched the thing over a hundred times?

4. *Heroes of the Alamo* (1937)
See above. Did I say bad? I mean *BAD.* But fascinating.

5. *The Alamo: 13 Days to Glory* (1987)
Bad costumes, no sense of period, an illogical and inaccurate script and cheesy production values. And those are the film's good points. The best awful scene in the film may be where the Alamo defenders crawl across the plain on their stomachs in order to sabotage some cannon. Luckily, the Mexican soldiers are looking the other way! This is to Alamo movies what *Plan 9 From Outer Space* is to science fiction. And it's still better than *James A. Michener's "Texas."*

* An exclusive entry for *The Alamo Almanac & Book of Lists.*

BEST ALAMO ACTORS*

In 1989 the members of the Alamo Society conducted a poll to determine the organization's favorite performers in Alamo movies. Here are the results:

Best Davy Crockett

#1 Fess Parker (*Davy Crockett, King of the Wild Frontier*)
#2 John Wayne (*The Alamo*)
#3 Arthur Hunnicutt (*The Last Command*)

Best William B. Travis

#1 Laurence Harvey (*The Alamo*)
#2 (tie) Richard Carlson (*The Last Command*)
　　　　 Alec Baldwin (*The Alamo: 13 Days to Glory*)

Best Jim Bowie

#1 Sterling Hayden (*The Last Command*)
#2 Kenneth Tobey (*Davy Crockett, King of the Wild Frontier*)
#3 Richard Widmark (*The Alamo*)

Best Santa Anna

#1 Raul Julia (*The Alamo: 13 Days to Glory*)
#2 Enrique Sandino (*Alamo . . . The Price of Freedom*)
#3 Ruben Padilla (*The Alamo*)

* An exclusive entry for *The Alamo Almanac & Book of Lists.*

TEXAS GOVERNORS WHO HAD
BROTHERS IN ALAMO MOVIES

Gov. Marion Price Daniel, Sr. (1957-1963)
Bill Daniel played Col. Neill in *The Alamo* (1960)

Gov. John B. Connally (1963-69)
Merrill Connally played Davy Crockett in *Alamo . . . The Price of Freedom* (1988)

FESS PARKER'S MOST MEMORABLE SCENES FROM "DAVY CROCKETT AT THE ALAMO"*

Fess Parker starred as Davy Crockett in the Walt Disney trilogy *Davy Crockett, King of the Wild Frontier* during the 1954-55 TV season. The final episode, "Davy Crockett at the Alamo" aired on February 23, 1955, coincidentally the 119th anniversary of the beginning of the Alamo's siege.

1. Singing "Farewell"
"The singing of 'Farewell' by Crockett and the men of the Alamo the night before the final battle is the scene that immediately comes to mind. It was a poignant moment for those men who were about to die. I think the scene was done well."

2. Drawing the Line
"The drawing of the line in the dirt by Colonel Travis (portrayed by Don Megowan) was an important moment. It was a fateful decision for those who crossed it."

3. Death of Bowie
"The death of Jim Bowie (portrayed by Kenneth Tobey) was a very powerful scene that demonstrated the courage of his character."

4. Crockett's Death
"That was a difficult scene to do, with all the stuntmen and everything. But it was handled well by Mr. Disney. For me, well, it was the end!"

* An exclusive entry for *The Alamo Almanac & Book of Lists.*

DAVID ZUCKER'S ALAMO TOUCHES
IN HIS *NAKED GUN* FILMS*

David Zucker is an accomplished film maker (*Airplane!;
Ruthless People; High School High*, among others) who direct-
ed/produced the popular *Naked Gun* comedies. Zucker, who
is also a collector of important historic Alamo and Davy
Crockett memorabilia, embellished his three *Naked Gun*
films with several Alamo and Crockett touches.

The Naked Gun: From the Files of Police Squad! (1989)
Not only is Lt. Frank Drebin's (Leslie Nielsen) apartment
filled with framed prints of the Alamo, Davy Crockett, and
Sam Houston, but a coonskin cap and a fringed, buckskin
jacket hang from the wall. In addition, 1824 flags were placed
atop a hospital entrance and a mock mid-Eastern palace. The
Alamo Society was even thanked in the credits!

The Naked Gun 2 1/2: The Smell of Fear (1991)
The film's opening sequence begins in a White House entrance hall that is embellished with large paintings of Sam
Houston and Davy Crockett, plus a reproduction of Onder-
donk's *The Fall of the Alamo*. A large John G. Chapman paint-
ing of Crockett is featured on the dining room wall. The
White House announcer is played by *Alamo Journal* editor
William Chemerka. Later in the film, an 1824 flag and a New
Orleans Greys flag border the American Stars and Stripes atop
a hotel entrance. The Alamo flags later appear at a police sta-
tion entrance as well. Zucker makes a cameo appearance as
Davy Crockett (along with Robert Weil who plays George
Russel) in a SWAT-team shootout scene!

Naked Gun 33 1/3: The Final Insult (1994)
A print of the Alamo chapel is the first historical wall hanging
seen in Lt. Frank Drebin's apartment. Three contemporary
prints of David Crockett (by artists John G. Chapman, James
H. Shegogue, and John Naegle) also adorn the walls. Of
course, a coonskin cap hangs from the wall as well!

* An exclusive entry for *The Alamo Almanac & Book of Lists*.

MOVIES FEATURING THE ALAMO FILMED AT ALAMO VILLAGE

Alamo Village is located on a ranch owned by the family of the late James T. "Happy" Shahan in Brackettville, Texas. The site got its name from John Wayne's *The Alamo*, which was filmed there in 1959. Alamo Village features dozens of eighteenth and nineteenth century-style buildings, including a cantina, a jail, stables, a bank, a blacksmith shop, a hotel, a general store, a church and, of course, the Alamo compound. The listed films were either films that dealt with the Siege and Battle of the Alamo (*Alamo . . . The Price of Freedom*, for example) or included at least one scene that featured the Alamo (*Lonesome Dove*). The production's release date follows each title. Those films marked with an asterisk (*) were primarily television productions.

The Alamo (1959)
Seguin (1980) *
Houston: The Legend of Texas (1986) *
The Alamo: 13 Days to Glory (1986) *
Alamo . . . The Price of Freedom (1987)
Lonesome Dove (1988) *
James Michener's "Texas" (1994) *

ACADEMY AWARD™ NOMINATIONS FOR JOHN WAYNE'S *THE ALAMO*

Category marked with an asterisk (*) indicates an Oscar™-winner from the Motion Picture Academy of Arts and Sciences.

Best Picture: (John Wayne, producer)

Best Supporting Actor: (Chill Wills as "The Beekeeper")

Color Cinematography: (William H. Clothier)

Editing: (Stuart Gilmore)

Music — Scoring of a Dramatic or Comedy Picture: (Dimitri Tiomkin)

Best Song: ("The Green Leaves of Summer" by Dimitri Tiomkin and Paul Francis Webster)

Sound: (Samuel Goldwyn Sound Department, Gordon E. Sawyer, sound editor; and Todd-AO Sound Department, Fred Hynes, Sound Editor)

MISSING SCENES FROM JOHN WAYNE'S *THE ALAMO*

In 1960 John Wayne released his epic motion picture, *The Alamo*. The film's initial road show print ran for 192 minutes. However, responses from a number of theater operators across the United States suggested that a shorter film would increase the number of daily showings. John Wayne reluctantly agreed, and in the autumn of 1960 he supervised the re-editing of *The Alamo*. The re-edited print, which was released to theaters in early 1961, ran for 161 minutes. For nearly thirty years, theater audiences (*The Alamo* was re-released in 1967) and home videocassette viewers saw an incomplete film.

The scenes listed below were not restored to the film until a copy of the original print was located and screened in a Toronto, Canada, theater on November 24, 1990. Subsequently, the so-called "Toronto Print" was returned to MGM/UA in California where it was restored and reissued in 1992 on videocassette.

* Reel #1, Part B: part of Bowie's initial scene
* Reel #2, Part A: Travis informs Bowie of the Alamo's command structure and sends Bonham for help

* Reel #2, Part B: Travis' Jeffersonian speech
* Reel #4, Part B: Crockett kills Sand in church
* Reel #5, Part A: Crockett informs Flaca of Sand's death
* Reel #5, Part A: Mrs. Guy's conversation with Flaca
* Reel #5, Part B: Smitty recalls skirmish
* Reel #5, Part B: Crockett's conversation with Bowie
* Reel #6, Part A: Crockett's conversation with Flaca
* Intermission Reel
* Reel #7, Part B: Texan's conversation with Smitty
* Reel #8, Part A: Travis' conversation with Bonham
* Reel #9, Part A: Alamo cattle patrol scene
* Reel #9, Part B: Arrival of Gonzales volunteers and Lisa
Dickinson's birthday party scene
* Reel #11, Part B: Beekeeper's statement about the
Parson
* Reel #12, Part A: Death of the Parson
* Reel #13, Part A: Finn's monologue and Tennesseans'
conversation
* Reel #14, Part A: part of Crockett's last stand

BIBLIOGRAPHY

Barr, Alwyn. *Texans in Revolt: The Battle of San Antonio 1835.* Austin: University of Texas Press, 1990.

Chariton, Wallace. *Exploring the Alamo Legends.* Plano, Texas: Wordware Publishing, Inc., 1990.

—*100 Days in Texas.* Plano, Texas: Wordware Publishing, Inc., 1990.

Daughters of the Republic of Texas. *The Alamo Long Barrack Museum.* Dallas: Taylor Publishing Co., 1986.

Groneman, Bill. *Alamo Defenders.* Austin: Eakin Press, 1990.

—*Defense of a Legend; Crockett and the de la Péna Diary.* Plano, Texas: Republic of Texas Press, 1994.

—*Eyewitness to the Alamo.* Plano, Texas: Republic of Texas Press, 1996.

Hardin, Stephen. *Texian Iliad, A Military History of the Texas Revolution.* Austin: University of Texas Press, 1994.

Lord, Walter. *A Time To Stand.* New York: Harper and Row Publishers, 1961.

Jackson, Ron. *Alamo Legacy: Alamo Descendants Remember the Alamo.* Austin: Eakin Press, 1997.

Matovina, Timothy M. *The Alamo Remembered, Tejano Accounts and Perspectives.* Austin: University of Texas Press, 1995.

Myers, John Myers. *The Alamo.* New York: E. P. Dutton & Co., 1948.

Nofi, Albert A. *The Alamo and the Texas War for Independence.* Conshohocken, Pennsylvania: Combined Books, Inc., 1992.

Schoelwer, Susan Prendergast. *Alamo Images, Changing Perceptions of a Texas Experience.* Dallas: DeGolyer Library and Southern Methodist University Press, 1985.

Thompson, Frank. *Alamo Movies.* East Berlin, Pennsylvania: East Berlin Press, 1991.

Tinkle, Lon. *13 Days To Glory; The Siege of the Alamo.* New York, Toronto and London: McGraw-Hill Book Co. Inc., 1958.

Todish, Tim J. *Alamo Sourcebook, 1836.* Austin: Eakin Press, 1997.